when TEXAS came for our KIDS

How evangelical extremists launched a war on *TRANSGENDER TEENS*

Riki Wilchins

For more information contact:
Riverdale Avenue Books
Magnus Books
5676 Riverdale Avenue
Riverdale, NY 10471
www.riverdaleavebooks.com

Design by www.formatting4U.com
Cover by Scott Carpenter.

Digital ISBN: 9781626016705
Print ISBN: 9781626016712

First edition, December 2023

Acknowledgements

Special thanks to Anne Georgulas, who was not only an invaluable source for context and fact-checking, but was the first person actually mentioned in this book to reach out and offer to speak with me. She was also the first person who encouraged me to write it, and was unerringly patient in letting me try out ideas and approaches for how to tell this story, even though she was still in the eye of the hurricane.

 Thanks also to Ximena Lopez, who provided invaluable background and context on GENECIS; and to Morgan Davis, Rachel Gonzales, and Brian Klosterboer of the Texas ACLU, each of whom corrected some of my more egregious errors of fact, while patiently helping me understand some the unique political currents of Texas. Brian was especially helpful in walking me through the intricacies of the various state lawsuits, and corrected my legal errors regarding them. I appreciated the insights of Texas Tribune journalist Roxanna Asgarian into both the work and the history of DFPS. The Guttmacher Institute kindly stepped me through locating their statistics on anti-abortion bills; Guttmacher continues to be an irreplaceable resource for reproductive health. Gillian Branstetter of the ACLU provided important background on media and communications.

My ever-patient researcher Chloe Souchere wrestled ACLU's data from 30 states and a dozen issues into manageable form, and Allie Gardner carefully corrected my hundreds of unformatted and often-incomplete footnotes—both were invaluable. With a text covering so many states, people, and actions over three decades years, I introduced many small errors of name, date, and number; Allison Hammond's detailed and careful fact-checking of each chapter saved me the ignominy of passing these on to the reader.

My personal thanks to the ACLU and Lambda Legal, who have tirelessly fought for the rights of transgender children, and to the dozens of parents across the south and west who were forced from their homes and jobs, and nonetheless took the time to share the stories of their transgender children and the personal toll the War on Trans Youth has taken on them and their families.

My special appreciation and thanks to legislative tracker Erin Reed for her tireless journalism which provided invaluable and irreplaceable context and detail for this book as many of its events were unfolding in real time—as evidenced by the many quotes from her "Erin in the Morning" blog that appear throughout the text.

Last of all, my heartful appreciation to my publisher, Lori Perkins of Riverdale Avenue Books, whose guidance, support, and friendship keep me writing.

Table of Contents

Dedication

To Gina and Dylan—you are my life.

A Word on Language

This book uses "trans" and "transgender" interchangeably. Trans is becoming increasingly common as way to indicate that the category remains unfinished and open to new identities. It also nods to a new time when a 2023 Washington Post/KFF poll found that those who are nonbinary, genderfluid, genderqueer, agender, etc. now form the majority of our community, only about one-third of whom still identify simply as "trans woman" or "trans man."[1] [2]

As the poll illustrates, the sheer breadth of those now sheltering under the well-known "transgender umbrella" creates challenges for any author hoping to write accurately about them. The poll also found that only 31% of those identifying as *transgender* or *trans* had undergone any kind of gender-affirming medical care.[3] However, the most virulent attacks have been reserved for the part of the community that does or wants to medically change their genders and/or bodies, and this book focuses on them. For instance, adult crossdressers have generally not been in the legislative crosshairs, nor have the many trans people who transition socially, but not medically (although some legislation is starting to target social transitions as well). Although many nonbinary, genderqueer, and genderfluid individuals also seek some sort of gendered body modification, I am unaware of them being specifically targeted by legislation. This is *not* to say that they aren't a part of this struggle or that their lives are not also under assault. Just that this book, which is about the growth of a specific kind of legislative and social war, has not focused on their unique struggles.

This book has a similar limitation when it comes to those trans youth who medically transition without a defined destination or body type in mind—usually articulated in terms of cisbody stereotypes[4] I realize that these chapters fail to do justice to those trans people who transition without such a defined, binary endpoint in mind, and also those who don't seek to present a stable and recognizable gender. I look forward to other books written by those better equipped than I to help us better understand how this hurtful crusade continues to harm them and their families. I do use the term "transsexual" rather than "transgender" in sections where I am specifically referring to those who seek to modify their body's primary and/or secondary sexual characteristics.

In the sections on bathrooms and sports, I have focused more on trans women, because the right has devoted the bulk of its animus and its attacks on them. There are many brilliant exceptions, like Gavin Grimm's determined fight for dignity in Virginia, and Mack Beggs' brave struggle to continue wrestling in Texas, even though the state forced him to wrestle against young women. But bathrooms and sports are areas where the transfemale body tends to be more socially controversial, and thus the preferred target of righting religious extremists. This is *not* to say that the bodies of trans men and boys are not also at risk, or that they don't feel similarly threatened: both are true.

In many cases I have used "trans children" and "trans kids" and "trans youth" interchangeably. I realize this is not always precise. Some pediatric affirming care—such as hormone blockers—are provided primarily to young people in their early adolescence to delay or pause the start of puberty.

Other forms of care—such as *top surgery*—are almost never provided at such early ages and solely to those in their later teens. Still other forms—such as bottom surgery—are almost never provided to minors of any age because they contravene the accepted medical Standards of Care followed by any reputable doctor. Despite this imprecision, I don't think it helps to continually remind the reader of this, especially since attacks almost never draw such distinctions and indeed habitually conflate all care with the canard that transitions inflict bottom surgery on prepubescent bodies.

Thus, I have tended to refer to transgender youth, transgender children, and transgender kids more or less interchangeably for young people under the age of 18. I have been a little wary of using the words "youth," or 'trans youth" in specific contexts, since "youth" is often considered to be older than "children" and starting around age 14, and many young people transition socially (or even begin blockers) prior to that age.

I have also spoken with lawyers representing families under attack for providing affirming care who make a point of using "transgender youth" to emphasize that medical care is only provided to adolescents, and not to those too young to have started puberty. I also realize that "children" or "kids" refers to a wide span of ages, from a six-year-old starting kindergarten to a 17-year-old on the verge of adulthood.

I trust that when referring to "transchildren" or "trans-kids" or "children" in discussion of blockers, hormones, or top surgery, that the reader will recognize that I am not referring any young person too young to properly receive them. In addition, although it is a colloquialism, my use of "kids" or "transkids" is in no way meant to be diminishing, must less to suggest a lack of respect for the brave efforts of those young people who are fighting for their lives in schools, local hearings, and legislative chambers. I simply employ it as a shorter, informal substitute for always writing "children."

Of the two dozen or so parents I interviewed who are providing affirming care, only one described their child as not being especially dysphoric and being comfortable with their body. Perhaps this is because her son had started hormone blockers immediately with the onset of puberty and was looking forward to top surgery at age 16. In any case, there are many others like him. However, this book's descriptions of what I call Endogenous Hormone Poisoning—having one's body forced through the wrong puberty—emphasizes the pain of dysphoria. Similarly, its political analysis is focused on those children who *are* highly dysphoric, who suffer extraordinarily from the withholding of care, and who are especially vulnerable to the crusade against pediatric care. I hope the readers will bear in mind and the imbalance in attention it creates.

I want to add that being dysphoric should not be confused with an unhappy childhood. The Washington Post/KFF poll found that about half of trans adults reported having a happy childhood, and that figure increased to almost two-thirds, when the person had a trusted adult who supported them. As Jules Gill-Peterson notes in the quote that opens the final chapter, a transgender childhood can be a happy and desirable one, rich and beautiful in its own way.

In those sections on banning gender-affirming medical care for young people, once the topic is introduced, I often simply refer to "care," or "affirming care," because the acronym "GAC" feels awkward and it does the reader a disservice to write out "pediatric gender-affirming care" over and over.

Similarly, it feels cumbersome to keep spelling out "participation in gender-appropriate school sports," so I often refer to "school sports" or more simply "sports." Except where specifically noted otherwise, all such references throughout this book are to young people, and not to transgender adults.

I have used "cisgender" to refer to those who are not transgender, and as a way of indicating that each of us— and not just those who are trans— are *doing* a gender.

Finally, having written about trans issues for some decades now, I have developed an unfortunate weakness for portmanteaus like "transcommunity" or "cispeople." I hope the reader will overlook this habit, and not let it distract from the important events it documents.

Riki Wilchins
November, 2023

Introduction

In early 2022, I began interviewing parents providing gender-affirming medical care to their transgender children. This was a relatively new phenomenon only a decade or so old. But there was already a startling divide between red and blue state parents. Those from states like New York or California had strikingly brief narratives in which their children came out, transitioned, were embraced by families and friends, got on blockers and progressed to hormones, and then went on with their lives. The End.

At the same time, I was talking with frantic parents who suddenly found themselves under attack from their own legislatures, who were making the care they were providing to their children a crime. Many (almost all of them single or divorced mothers) were in the midst of giving up their homes and careers to flee states like Georgia, Idaho, and Texas. Their stories quickly became the focus of the book. When I had first begun thinking about the project, pediatric gender-affirming care was still common and available in all 50 states. By the time I finished, anti-trans bills by the hundreds had been introduced into dozens of state legislatures.

I realized there was another story to be documented, and this book is the result. Part I sets background and historical context; Part II documents the first successful assault on trans youth as it happened, with insights from the parents, activists, lawyers, and doctors who were in the front-lines. Much of Part II unfolded in real-time, with events happening as I was writing them—often so quickly, and on so many fronts, that I struggled to keep up.

Eventually I realized the book needed an endpoint, even if the struggle it documented was ongoing. I chose December 31st, 2022, by which time Texas had implemented the nation's first effective ban on pediatric gender-affirming medical care. At that point, the origins of the right's attack, its strategies and main players, and its ultimate endpoints could also all be seen clearly and in their entirety. So many bills had been introduced that within a few months, the drumbeat of new bills had largely sputtered out, and the struggle has shifted largely to the federal courts.

This is something entirely new in American politics, and no one knows how it will end. This book is the untold story of why it happened and how it came to be.

Part I
Beginnings

Chapter 1 — Origins of a Tribal Crusade

Sometime in the early 2020s, transgender people, and not just trans people generally but the activities of transgender young people—what they wore, the games they played, their names and pronouns, the bathrooms they used, even their physical pubescent bodies—came to bear an enormous political importance, transforming in a matter of mere months from a non-issue into topic of national attention which dominated state legislatures, media cycles, and the policy platforms of one of the country's two major political parties.

It quickly became a core issue in the Presidential campaigns of the two leading Republican candidates, as Ron DeSantis and Donald Trump each made attacking transgender youth centerpieces of both their campaigns, even releasing simultaneous attack ads on the same day: DeSantis gaudily condemning "hacking off body parts," and Trump denouncing medical care for kids as "ridiculous," "mutilation," "madness" and "left-wing gender insanity."[5] [6] The genders of a few thousand children had become a defining issue in the 2024 presidential stakes and by extension, the future of the country.

In the two and a quarter years from January 2021 to April 2023, legislators in 42 of the 50 states introduced almost 1,000 anti-transgender bills—about 500 in the first quarter of 2023 alone, the vast majority of which specifically targeted transgender youth.[7] [8]

As another phase of the right's endless anti-gay culture war, this was distinctly different. Homosexuality was essentially a private practice between adults, so legislative assaults had been mainly confined to sexual practice (anti-sodomy law), dress (mostly enforced against lesbians), marriage rights, and military service.

But one's gender is public: it is tracked by multiple government, medical, and educational entities; and altering it physically entities who must be licensed by the state, such as doctors and therapists. All of this provided rightwing legislators nearly limitless points of attack: birth certificate, legal name and sex; driver's license; medical and psychiatric therapy care; sports; bathrooms; dress codes; pronouns; school; foster care; prison policies; insurance and Medicaid reimbursement; pharmaceutical companies; medical and hospital licensure; and on and on.

As 2022 drew to a close and the assault reached its crescendo, so many bills were being introduced regarding so many issues that—in order to avoid being trampled in the rush to subdue the threat posed by transgender children—legislators in Missouri, Montana, New Hampshire, Oklahoma, South Carolina, Tennessee, Texas, Virginia, and Utah took to pre-filing their anti-trans bills for 2023.[9] [10] In Montana alone, with a transgender youth population of only a few hundred kids, four bills were pre-filed, and many more were introduced as the year commenced.[11] In some legislatures, business virtually ground to a halt, as multiple hearings were launched to oversee one anti-trans bill or another.

As this book hopes to show, this assault on trans youth

was always intended to be just the opening move in rekindling the lapsed war on homosexuality. For example, after passing a number of anti-trans laws, Tennessee would pass the nation's first law criminalizing gay drag shows. Gov. Bill Lee signed the legislation, even after the press produced colleges pictures of *him doing drag*.[12] Asked about this minor incongruity, Lee seethed, "[it's] ridiculous... conflating something like that to sexualized entertainment in front of children."[13] [14] A banner immediately went up over the main bridge to Nashville, the state capital, thanking Lee for his "tireless work to fight trannies and fags"... accompanied by a Nazi swastika.[15] [16] [17] [18]

It is perhaps no coincidence that Tennessee is also the birthplace of the Ku Klux Klan, the state with the highest population of white evangelicals, and the single most active state in attacking transgender children. The ultra-rightwing Manhattan Institute would hyper-ventilate that "the drag queen might appear a comic figure, but he carries an utterly serious message: the deconstruction of sex, the reconstruction of child sexuality, and the subversion of middleclass family life [based on an] ideology born in the sex dungeons of San Francisco...."[19] The author of this screed was none other than reputed rightwing bigot Christopher Rufo, who has been credited with initiating the rightwing backlash against Critical Race Theory, and was now trying to use drag queens to smear both gays by encouraging the right to refer to them as "trans strippers," to make them "lurid" and "sexual."[20] [21]

Perhaps unaware that kids' bodies don't produce sex hormones before puberty (which is what *makes it* puberty), Tennessee's bill would outlaw hormone treatments for prepubescent youth, which was like outlawing private ownership of unicorns. According to a *Washington Post* analysis, by early 2023, Tennessee would distinguish itself in the coming religious crusade against transgender youth by passing no less than *seven laws* in total—at that point the most in the nation— out of 25 bills its legislature introduced.[22]

Even so, Tennessee would lose whatever demented race was underway to Iowa, where the legislature introduced 26 anti-trans bills—only one of which it was enacted into law—and to North Dakota, which, with a population of trans kids estimated to be 5,000—would advance no less than 10 anti-trans bills (eight to the governor's desk) in a single day, at the time a national record.[23] [24] [25]

Analyzing data provided by the ACLU, researcher Chloe Souchere and I found that the sheer volume of bills introduced targeting trans youth doubled in 2020 and again in 2021. Two thousand twenty-one was the turning point, with more bills introduced than in the previous *three years combined.*[26] By 2023 things really went batshit, and more anti-transgender bills were introduced in the first half of 2023 than in the entire legislative history of the U.S. This was exceeded only by the introduction of *even more* anti-abortion bills, often by the same legislators in the same states—showing how closely the two issues are linked in the white evangelical Christian mind.[27] These were followed closely behind by a flood of somewhat fewer voter suppression bills. (See Appendix A).

It was maelstrom of such reckless cruelty that it left the transgender children and their families trapped in its crosshairs bewildered and frightened, wondering when— or even if—it would ever end.[28] [29] Trans kids in more than one state, watching their lives being demonized by their own representatives, would attempt to take their lives.

The first round of anti-trans bills targeted school

sports, but the right openly bragged that it was always intended to be a stalking horse for a much bigger target; criminalizing gender-affirming care (GAC). From 2018 through 2022, Republican legislatures in almost half the states (22) introduced 79 measures making affirming care for young people a crime.[30] As proof of just how much animus there was towards gender medical care, almost a third of these (23) would become law—this was nearly three times the average for anti-trans bills, about 10% of which actually passed on average.

Kentucky's HB 470, which sought to roll every conceivable attack into a single bill, provided a kind of snapshot of the kind of imaginative cruelty being brought to bear.[31] It included not only the now-familiar prohibitions—medical care, birth certificate changes, school sports, insurance reimbursement—but also made it illegal for schools to allow transkids to use their proper names, pronouns, and clothing, or for schools to fail to notify parents if their child displayed gender noncon-forming behaviors, or for any adult to fail to alert law enforcement if a family was *known or suspected* of providing their child trans medical care. About the only thing HB 470 left out was branding transgender children with a scarlet letter and having them pilloried in the town stocks so they could be publicly stoned by passersby.

None of this prevented the bill's lead sponsor, Rep. Jennifer Decker (R-Waddy KY), and her 20 co-sponsors from naming it the "Do No Harm Act" (Decker, perhaps not coincidentally, ran a women's Christian homeless shelter and led its weekly Bible study group).[32] [33] [34]

HB 470 and many other bills like it were little more than an exercise in legislative excess, ranging from the dubious legality to outright unconstitutionality, and were totally unpassable even in Republican-dominated states. Often their own sponsors would freely admit that they knew of no actual problem their bills might remedy.

But remedy was not the point, which was more along the lines of what disability scholars have called *eugenics policymaking*, in which the state seeks to dictate which kinds of human life are acceptable and which aren't, and then to legislate the latter out of existence by removing their rights, erasing them administratively, and generally denying them the social and legal resources needed to survive.[35] [36]

By early 2023, it was possible to see in this campaign the emerging outlines of possible overreach, sense a *fin de siècle,* as rightwing extremists began testing the limitations of how many inventive ways a vindictive majority could wreck its legislative control on a disfavored few. And as often happens in these lemming-like pile-ons by the right, the sheer excess of its malice started to veer into farce.

For instance, Florida directed its High School Athletic Association to re-issue its Preparticipation Physical Evaluation form with a new Females Only section containing a plethora of intimate questions: *When was your first menstrual period? When was your most recent menstrual period? How much time do you usually have from the start of one period to the start of another? How many periods have you had in the last year? What was the longest time between periods in the last year?* Its only apparent purpose was intimidating the state's tiny handful of transfemale athletes, and it was eventually withdrawn.[37] [38]

North Dakota introduced legislation that would fine its citizens $1,500 for each public use of a trans person's name or pronoun that was inconsistent with their "deoxyribonucleic acid" (DNA).[39] A similar Montana bill would make such use illegal, but only in government buildings.

But it was another North Dakota bill that provided signs of the crusades coming legislative exhaustion, as rightwing extremists began falling for their own disinformation with HB 1522, which sought to ban schools from accommodating transgender students who claimed to be a member of *a non-human species.*[40]

That is not a misprint. Apparently missing the email that not everything on social media is 100% true, legislators fell for a hoax video from the anti-trans hate group, Moms for Liberty, in which a member accused a Michigan Public School of providing litterboxes for transgender students who identified as cats and dogs. The superintendent immediately denied this, asserting quite sensibly that there had "never been litterboxes within MPS schools."[41]

But the cat was out of the bag.

Similar rightwing hoaxes had floated around for years, but this one was picked up by bad-boy, wing-nut podcaster Joe Rogan and the virulently anti-gay Twitter account, *Libs of TikTok*—and it quickly went viral.

The video's apparent intent was trolling transgender people over how absurd it was to assert that one had changed sexes, much as the rabidly anti-trans cartoon *South Park* had notoriously compared it to changing into a porpoise or a Black person.[42] But since 2+2 always equals 22 in the rightwing echo chamber, predictably it didn't end there, and it didn't end well.

Tennessee state representatives were the next to cite the "growing crisis." Rep. Lauren Boebert, one of Colorado's eight Representatives to the US House of Representatives, warned of "litter boxes in schools for people who identify as cats." In Illinois, a Republican nominee for Congress tweeted about students using litterboxes, adding breathlessly: "Many parents and teachers have confided in me privately about the madness that's happening…."[43]

In Colorado, Heidi Ganahl, a 2022 GOP candidate for governor, claimed on state-wide television that there were "30 different schools" in which transkids were "…mute, and they don't talk: they growl and meow. It's bizarre. That's an extreme example, but it's happening." When called on this obvious falsehood, Ganahl would double-down, declaring she had heard this from "over 100 parents."[44]

In Minnesota's legislature litterboxes were cited to justify banning trans students from using the proper school restrooms. And *then* it got weird. Scott Jensen, Minnesota's Republican *nominee for Governor* and *a practicing physician*, would demand to know: "What are we doing to our kids? Why are we telling elementary kids that they get to choose their gender this week? Why do we have litterboxes in some of the school districts so kids can pee in them, because they identify as a furry? We've lost our minds. We've lost our minds."

Indeed "we" had.[45] [46]

Finally, in one mercilessly mocked video, Nebraska State Senator Bruce Bostelman publicly accused local schools of promoting an unsanitary environment for students to do their bodily elimination:

"It's something that kind of took me back just a little bit. And I'm a little shocked I guess is what I would put it.

It's something called 'furries.' If you don't know what furries are, it's where school children dress up as animals, cats or dogs, during the school day, they meow and they bark, and they interact with their school with the teachers and that in this fashion. And now schools are wanting to put litterboxes in the schools for these children to use. How is this sanitary?"[47]

"Furry-dom" is actually an adult costume play ("cosplay") subculture in which followers dress up as anthropomorphic animals like well-known cartoon characters (think Goofy at Disneyland, but for fun instead of pay).[48] It has nothing do with gender or with children. But this did not stop Bostelman from demanding an explanation from Nebraska's schools about unsanitary litterboxes—although it did inform his later apology and retraction.

Unwilling to be out-crazied, back in North Dakota, a local school board began accusing trans-species students of being walked to their classes on leashes. And in Texas, Michelle Evans, the Republican candidate for the U.S. House of Representatives, claimed that cafeteria tables were being lowered so that students who identified as cats and dogs could "more easily eat without utensils or their hands."

All of these would be among the nearly two dozen prominent Republican politicians—from local school board members all the way up to candidates for the governor's mansion—citing the growing *crisis* of trans kids barking and meowing, and doing their daily elimination in school-supplied litterboxes.[49] [50] [51]

It was, in other words, a certifiable rightwing feeding frenzy—and it would have been amusing had it not fed on the lives, hopes, and dysphoria of transgender children.[52] Shocked by the speed and finality with which a Supreme Court packed with ultra-conservatives justices had legalized sodomy and gay marriage, and then—only one year later—outlawed discrimination against LGBTQ+ people, the evangelical Christian nationalist right had trained the full fire of its rage on a group of children who were now the centerpiece of its culture war agenda.[53] As the *New York Times* explained:

> *Defeated on same-sex marriage, the religious right went searching for an issue that would re-energize supporters and donors. The campaign that followed stunned political leaders across the spectrum.*
>
> *When the Supreme Court declared a constitutional right to same-sex marriage nearly eight years ago, social conservatives were set adrift.*
>
> *The ruling stripped them of an issue they had used to galvanize rank-and-file supporters and big donors. And it left them searching for a cause that — like opposing gay marriage — would rally the base and raise the movement's profile on the national stage.*
>
> *We knew we needed to find an issue that the candidates were comfortable talking about,"* said Terry Schilling, the president of American Principles Project, a social conservative advocacy group. *"And we threw everything at the wall."*
>
> *What has stuck, somewhat unexpectedly, is the issue of transgender identity, particularly among young people.*[54]

So, they would seize on transkids, fundamentalist right's "last foothold in the fight against expanding LGBTQ+. Rights."[55] And in their fury, they reached for deadly firepower. It was like using a Howitzer to kill a butterfly.[56] The War on Trans youth would grow faster and more inhumane than either side could have imagined. It was as if the very idea of adolescents trying to change their sex was so disorienting, so dislocating to the fundamentalist evangelical mind and its commitment to the procreative, heterosexual nuclear family, that suddenly anything seemed possible—even children being walked on leashes, mooing or woofing and identifying as cats or dogs... or pet rocks. It was as if stumbling into modernity had unhinged the evangelical Christian mind.

But this War not a Republican one, although legislatively it is waged exclusively by Republican politicians. Nor was it even, strictly speaking, a political war, although it is being fought by passing state laws. This is not a political war for votes or a fight over laws and public policies. It is a white, evangelical Christian nationalist crusade against secular civil society itself, with the goal of imposing a nation of Biblically-ordained families, sexes, and genders.

Although no major news outlet is willing to call it that.

As AFL-CIO Political Director Michael Podhorzer notes, "the weaponization of right-wing Christianity is the elephant in the room." And the media's refusal to name it "hides from view the enormous influence wielded in our politics today by faith leaders who weaponize their faith..."[57] So the media dodge, and simply call it *extremism*. But as researcher Frederick Clarkson notes,

"[T]here's no wiggling out of it. In this area, it's the biggest failure in American journalism."[58]

About the closest any mainstream outlet will come to naming the issue is an Associated Press story carefully titled, "Christian Nationalism on the Rise in Some GOP Campaigns." The lead graph opens: "The victory party took on the feel of an evangelical worship service after Doug Mastriano won Pennsylvania's Republican gubernatorial primary this month. As a Christian singer led the crowd in song, some raised their arms toward the heavens in praise. Mastriano opened his remarks by evoking Scripture…Let's choose this day to serve the Lord.'"[59]

The A/P article cited 2022 Idaho gubernatorial hopeful Lt. Gov. Janice McGeachin, who posted a video of herself next to the American flag, holding a Bible in one hand and a .45 automatic in the other, while declaring: "God calls us to pick up the sword and fight, and Christ will reign in the state of Idaho." (Biblical scholars have long noted the paucity of mentions in the New Testament of automatic weapons.)

McGeachin's video is a near-perfect encapsulation of the core ideals of white evangelical Christian nationalism, which weaponizes Jesus' message of radical love for others, personal sin, and the need for personal salvation into a fierce intolerance for outsiders, the sinfulness of society, and the need for an American salvation that can only be met by officially becoming (by force if necessary) a Christian nation.

In an article titled "Christian Nationalism Is Authentically Christian," ex-evangelical journalist Chrissy Stroop echoed Clarkson's frustration with media "actively struggling with not wanting to face the fact that white evangelical support for Trump makes perfect sense with respect to White evangelicals' version of the Christian faith…and to the corollary notions that 'real' Christians' could [be] authoritarians and insurrectionists…"[60] [61] [62]

This media naming embargo continued even after Michael Podhorzer—a former AFL-CIO Political Director whom Time magazine credits as "the architect [of the] shadow campaign that saved the 2020 Election"—published a blistering in-depth analysis titled, "Hiding in Plain Sight," which documented with numerous charts and graphs the full extent of the white Christian nationalist rights' massive political organizing machine.[63]

Clarkson, Stroop, and Podhorzer are right.

Mainstream media *does* want to avoid using religious terminology, and they do. Americas have a long tradition of avoiding religion in politics, and we tend to be uncomfortable basing political arguments on someone's religion or religious belief. In fact, I'm not entirely comfortable doing it here either: it smacks of religious intolerance. It is reminiscent of the viciously anti-Catholic campaign of the 1960's against John F. Kennedy, claiming that as president, he would be little more than the Vatican's puppet. Such attacks are abhorrent, especially in a country whose founders included many fleeing religious prosecution at home.

Americans tend to want to base their political conflicts around people's public statements and actions, not on how they worship. Or as Queen Elizabeth I put it much more eloquently, "We have no desire to make windows into men's souls."

But this discomfort with mixing religion with

politics has created an enormous blind spot among the left, which fails to fully grapple with the War on Trans youth in part because it resists identifying it accurately. It is actually less a religion or religious affiliation than an ethnic tribal identity.[64] [65] [66] As evangelical theologian Russell Moore has pointed out, white Christian nationalism (WCN) itself can be considered anti-Christian, since it substitutes connection with in-group identity for a personal connection with God.[67] As such, Christian nationalism is more a political affiliation than a matter of faith.

Among the 10 more extreme states in passing draconian anti-trans legislation are eight of the 15 states that have passed the most draconian anti-abortion laws, even forbid exceptions even for rape and incest.[68] The same group which drafted the Mississippi abortion ban that led to the overturning of *Roe v. Wade* is now leading the lawsuit seeking to overturn women's rights to mifepristone, one of the two medications needed for a successful medical abortion.[69]

Tennessee, which has introduced more anti-LGBTQ+ bills than any other state (48), also leads in the percentage of its population who identify as white evangelical Christians, (52%.)[70] It also enacted the nation's most stringent abortion ban, which forces women to carry fetuses which have lethal anomalies and/or are dead *in utero* to term.[71] [72] Also not co-incidentally, according to the Southern Poverty Law Center, Tennessee has more paramilitary hate groups *per capita* than any other state except Montana.[73] [74]

On the left, we fight anti-abortion and anti-transgender struggles separately, but they are twin forks in the struggle to impose Scriptural control over our bodily autonomy. This should be impossible in a functional democracy. But white evangelical nationalism is authoritarian as well, seeking to overthrow of liberal democracy and replace it with a nation ruled by Biblical principles.

For all the far right's hyperventilating about imaginary efforts by Islamic fundamentalists to impose Sharia law in America, *they* are the ones actively seeking to impose an anti-democratic religious regime. The top 15 states in passing anti-transgender laws include almost all of the eight states that have passed anti-democratic bills empowering Republican officials to overturn elections, they also include almost all of the nine that states that have imposed the most extreme voter suppression laws.[75] [76] [77] [78] And they are among the states which have the most attacks by paramilitary extremist groups that seek to impose by violence what they have been unable to win at the ballot box.

Transgender rights, abortion rights, Black voting rights, preserving democratic institutions—they are but different facets of a common religious crusade against modern, secular America. Daniel Patrick Moynihan was famous for observing that *we are entitled to our own opinion, but we are not entitled to our own facts.* But now this no longer applies: white Christian nationalists have their own reality and their own "alternative facts" — and both are radically incompatible with liberal, multi-ethnic democracy.[79]

We are in the midst of a slow-burning second Civil War, being fought at the ballot box, the pew, in state legislatures, and increasingly (by WCN paramilitaries) in the streets. Although the animating force behind WCN is white Christian supremacy, this war is not over the vile

17

institutions of lynching and chattel slavery, but over the existence of democratic civil society itself.[80]

Although WCN may seem new, it is just a modern version of the paranoid Christian right's historic hostility to Black Americans, immigrants, Jews, Catholics, civil rights, homosexuality, reproductive rights, secularism, and women's voting.[81] It has been stitched into the very fabric of white Protestant ascendency since Plymouth Rock.[82] [83] It is as American as apple pie. Yet as with all large movements, labels conceal considerable complexity and overlap.

Evangelical Christianity is not a denomination but a religious movement whose core principles include belief in the Bible as the word of God, the centrality of personal spiritual conversion (being "born-again"), and converting non-believers.

White Christian nationalism is a political and religious conviction that the U.S. was founded as a white Christian nation, and that Christians are chosen by God to remake America according to Biblical principles to be an example for the rest of the world. It is characterized by the use of Christian symbolism, slogans, and teachings to promote what is essentially an ethnic racial identity centered on white Protestant male ascendancy.[84]

Although WCN is overwhelming an evangelical movement, neither it nor evangelicalism, are uniform.

- About 1-in-4 white evangelicals are unsupportive of white Christian nationalism.
- A substantial minority of white Christian nationalists are not evangelical but Pentecostal, Catholic, or Mormon.[85] [86]

- There are Christian nationals who are not white but Black and Latinx and who also seek a Biblically-inspired America, just not a white-dominated one.
- Not all white evangelicals are anti-LGBTQ+: 38% support gay marriage, and 62% say they favor workplace nondiscrimination protection for LGBTQ+ people.[87] [88]

Yet if the correlation between ideological affiliation and religious belief is imperfect, it is nonetheless unmistakable. A 2023 PRRI/Brookings Institution poll found that more than half of Republicans are (54%) supporters of WCN, compared to just 23% of independents and 15% of Democrats.[89]

And among white evangelicals alone, PRRI found that nearly two-thirds (64%) express support for Christian nationalism. In their book, *Taking America Back for God*, sociologists Andrew Whitehead and Samuel Perry found the even more alarming figure of 78%.[90] [91] Whatever the exact figure, white evangelicals are the only major denomination in which a majority consistently support Christian nationalism.[92]

Support is not only high among white evangelical church-goers than any other denomination, it is even higher among the many "unchurched" white evangelical Christian nationalists, who have fashioned their own idiosyncratic, Christian-themed belief systems (think the bare-chested, horn-helmeted, flag-wearing QAnon Shaman from January 6's attack on the U.S. Capitol)[93] [94]

Evangelicalism itself appears to be incubating white Christian nationalism and *vice versa*. And its uniformity of belief combined with the blending of religious with political belief has enabled the WCN groups to transform thousands of evangelical churches into a mass *get out the vote* network for the right, successfully skirting laws that prohibit politics in the pulpit.[95] As reporter Katherine Stewart argues in *Faith Militant*, his huge, disciplined network, combined the hundreds of millions of dollars funding an army of organizations has effectively transformed white Christian nationalists into "a shadow political party" that operates from within the shell of what used to be the GOP.[96]

Among white Christian nationalist evangelicals, religion is not a way of worship and drawing closer to God, but rather a means of accumulating political power and dominating nonbelievers. As a belief system, it is perpetually aggrieved, religiously intolerant, inherently racist, and supremacist in its ambitions.[97][98]

Philip Gorski and Samuel Perry argue in their book, *The Flag and the Cross*, that the U.S. cannot be both a white Christian nation *and* a diverse democracy. As Trump's National Security Advisory Michael Flynn put it succinctly: "[W]e have to have one religion, one nation under God and one religion under God, right?"—underscoring WCN assertions that US is not based on the Constitutional consent of the governed, but on the Biblical word of God.[99][100]

But *Taking America Back for God* found that 70% of Americans do not want the U.S. to officially become a Christian country, and 73% want the U.S. to be diverse society.[101]

So, in order to pursue their vision of white, Christian America evangelical nationalists are increasingly turning against majority-rule democracy, embracing a range of anti-democratic means that includes threats and violence from white Christian nationalist paramilitaries like the

Three Percenters, Proud Boys, Patriot Front, and Oath Keepers.[102] [103]

This is the force that is animating the War on Trans youth.

In effect, an entire segment of society across the South and West was silently seething over the very existence of gay and trans people and—combined with the actions of its own Supreme Court—was wounded and enraged beyond reason. Red states with large evangelical white populations, working closely with well-funded Christian nonprofits and mega donors, began identifying every legal *and* extra-legal means of making the lives of their tiny populations of transgender children unlivable.

As Adam Serwer noted in, "The Cruelty Is the Point," it was the kind of performative cruelty towards women, children, and minorities that is the proud trademark of the Trumpist Christian nationalist right.[104]

And it seemed to come out of nowhere. As legislative blogger Erin Reed pointed out, if a time machine whisked us back to 2020, the lives of transgender children in half the country would be virtually unrecognizable. Just three short years ago, they could change names and pronouns, update birth certificates, transition genders, and obtain puberty blockers or hormones freely and legally in all 50 states without comment or attention, much less political back-lash.[105] Because it's such an excellent summary, it is worth quoting her blog post at length [*edited for brevity – ED.*]:

> *[I]t is clear that this was a coordinated strategy from the right to use sports and bathrooms to usher in a new era of anti-trans oppression. It was never about sports, it was never about bathrooms: elimination was always*

the end goal... The fallout of the anti-trans bathroom bills halted legislative attacks on transgender rights for four years. During the Trump presidency, there were a handful of executive actions targeting the transgender community, but things were relatively quiet at the state level. For anti-trans groups, though, they were regrouping and building out their legislative strategy for the future—a strategy which we have seen play out for the last three years. In 2019, a conservative group called the American Principles Project, which refers to itself as the "NRA for families," released its first anti-trans advertisement to ban transgender people from sports in Kentucky.

This was the opening salvo of the modern attack on transgender rights:

At the same time, the Christian conservative organization Alliance Defending Freedom... began a relentless series of legal attacks on the transgender community. ADF took up a case in Connecticut of three cisgender girls suing to have two transgender girls banned from competition. This lawsuit met its final failure in December of 2022. These two organizations would become central to the reactionary push to curtail transgender rights in the following years, and we are finally feeling the full effects of the strategy they developed during the attacks on transgender sports today.

In 2020, we saw the first anti-sports bills introduced following the Connecticut athlete lawsuit and the ads run by American Principles

Project. Idaho passed the first sports ban in 2020. It also passed a bill banning the changing of birth certificates to match a transgender person's gender identity. Both of these bills were later blocked in court, but it represented the first victory for these anti-trans groups. Sports Illustrated reported at the time that the draft of this bill was provided by ADF. Meanwhile, APP started adding transgender healthcare in their advertisements with an ad targeted at Joe Biden for "endorsing gender change treatments for minors."[106]

This was all part of a very deliberate strategy to expand the targeting of trans people to new arenas.

The following year, 2021, was the year that legislative attacks in the transgender community exploded.

Tennessee enacted a bathroom sign law that made establishments post a warning if they allowed trans people in bathrooms. Montana banned updates to birth certificates without surgery. Seven states passed anti-trans sports bans. This was also the year that we saw our first healthcare ban passed. ADF and APP were working behind the scenes on all of this. The Washington Post reported that the language was drafted by conservative groups like the Heritage Foundation, the Eagle Forum, and ADF...

A total of 18 states banned transgender participation in sports—many of these bills were supported and drafted by ADF as reported by the USA Today. American Principles

Project focused millions of dollars in campaign ads on those same sports bans going into the 2022 midterms. In an interview with CNN, the president of APP drew out exactly how they enacted this series of anti-trans legislation that we are seeing continue to grow today.

The "sports issue" was only ever meant as a way to make anti-trans policies more palatable to legislators… "The women's sports issue was really the beginning point in helping expose all this because what it did was, it got opponents of the LGBT movement comfortable with talking about transgender issues."[107]

APP next targeted explicitly business-friendly states such as Florida and Texas because they would be difficult to boycott.[108] CNN also reported that this organization has continued to work with legislators on anti-trans initiatives in other states. Three years after the APP launched the first part of its plan focused on women's sports, it is now clear that their strategy has seen some success… [APP claims that] the debate over gay marriage was a sham and that 'essentially we went from Obergefell and gay marriage to now sex changes for gay minors, hormone treatments, and puberty blockers.'

Reed's comments are echoed by the ACLU's Chase Strangio, who noted how restricting trans people's medical rights has shifted "incredibly far…in a way that was completely unfathomable to many of us even just three or four years ago,"[109]

To white evangelical nationalist groups like ADF and APP who planned and prosecuted war, it was neither sudden nor or unfathomable: it was meant to happen this way. It was the result of a well-thought out and deliberate campaign which identify and then exploit key vulnerabilities in the left's ambivalent feelings about transgender children and their bodies in order to reignite the culture wars.[110] The effort was reportedly bankrolled by a common group of deep-pocketed billionaire funders and donors such as:

- Reported rightwing ideologue Sean Fieler, the chair of APP, and reportedly it's largest single donor.[111] [112] Fieler is also reportedly the largest single supporter of anti-gay marriage efforts, and—even in the wake of *Obergefell*—reportedly remains fully committed to overturning gay marriage.[113]
- The evangelical National Christian Charitable Foundation, whose nearly $5b in assets make it one of the world's largest foundations and which has provided ADF with $86m over just six years
- The evangelical Servant Foundation, which is reportedly ADF's largest single funder and which has funded the $100m national *He Gets Us* campaign devoted to "rebranding Jesus" as one who *loves those we hate* (presumably not including transgender children).[114] [115] [116]
- Reportedly rightwing ideologue David Green, founder of Hobby Lobby.[117] Hobby Lobby ("honoring the Lord ...by operating ...with Biblical principles") famously won a Supreme Court case which made it legal for corporations to refuse reproductive health services to (female) employees

because of their religious belief (a real-life example of Mitt Romney's absurd comment that "corporations are people").[118] Green is also reportedly the key funder behind Kentucky's Creation Museum (which shows humans and dinosaurs cavorting together a few thousand years before the birth of Christ), and DC's Museum of the Bible (which has since been exposed for promoting a major collection of Dead Sea Scrolls which proved to be fake).[119] [120] [121]

- And reported rightwing extremist Dick Uihlein, who contributed more than $5.5 million or 80% of APP PAC's budget for attack ads last year—much of it devoted to anti-transgender attack ads.[122] [123] [124]

As Mark Rozell and Clyde Wilcox document in their study, "Second Coming: The Strategies of the New Christian Right," such groups are an outgrowth of 1970s white evangelical groups like Jerry Falwell's "Moral Majority," which sought to move beyond the televangelism of preachers Billy Graham and Pat Robertson. This New Christian Right sought to marry the spiritual devotion of evangelical worshippers with the secular needs of Republican politics.[125] But early NCR groups failed: they were intolerant of non-Christians, employed harsh religious messages, and built no real political infrastructure.[126]

As a result, by 2018, only few isolated legislators had introduced a handful of anti-trans bills favored by NCR groups, and they had gone nowhere.

But newer groups like Family Research Council, Heritage, APP, and ADF had spent three decades investing in infrastructure, build a well-organized, motivated, and coordinated national movement.[127] They brought with them sophisticated packaging, model legislation, poll-tested secular messaging, and tens of millions of dollars of funding. It was a game-changer, reversing a long string of defeats on LGBTQ+ rights overnight and turning a minor issue into a national rallying cry, an essential part of rightwing identity.[128] You could hardly be real Republican, until you had introduced your own bill anti-transgender bill.

It was a religious crusade, a nationwide moral panic. And it was devastatingly effective.[129]

This is the untold story behind how this crusade was planned and launched, the reasons transgender kids were selected as its target, and the weaknesses on the left that it identified and then ruthlessly exploited.

It is the story of how transgender young people suddenly found themselves thrust into the frontlines of the rights' endless battles against *homosexuality.* Becoming overnight *the* pre-eminent culture war issue of the 2020s, rivaled only by abortion and immigration.

It is also the story of how the American public began to grapple for first time with the realities of behind the sensationalized phrase "changing sex," and what forcing an adolescent to undergo the wrong puberty does to their bodies, and the sheer desperation of many to avoid that fate.

And it is the story of how Texas Republicans took the rights of their transgender children captive, competing with one another to promote the harshest measure, finally enacting the first ban on gender affirming care in our nation's history through blatantly extra-legal, unconstitutional means—all in service of whipping up their white evangelical Christian extremist base for the 2020 primary.

In 1999 when the Gender Public Advocacy Coalition (GenderPAC) launched the annual National Gender Lobby Day, the idea of trans people being out and in public—much less lobbying Congress for civil rights—was underheard of. Trans people were considered a small, bizarre social fringe. Our public profile was mostly lurid articles in the *National Enquirer* or shock appearances on The Jerry Springer Show, and serious dialog about transsexuals and crossdressers (the word "transgender" was very new) was mostly confined to psychiatric texts or feminist academic journals.

Even within the trans community, being transgender was still considered a personal rather than political issue. Crossdressers mostly wanted safe places to dress, and transsexuals mostly wanted to transition and get on with their lives. The fact that neither could do so without being fired, harassed, or attacked was seen as a personal failing because of not "passing" rather than a matter of civil rights. And this was reflected in the many transgender conferences held around the country each year, which were among the earliest gatherings for trans people. For instance, a "Be All You Can Be" guide from the 1990s listed workshops like *Make-over Lessons; What Am I & Where Am I Going?; Is Coming Out for Me?; Do's and Don'ts of Going Out;* and *Wives and Women of Crossdressers.* There was nothing on politics, organizing, or civil rights.[130]

About the only time GenderPAC received any mainstream media or political attention was when an adult transgender woman (and it was always a woman) transitioned and a city or corporation decided to allow her to use the proper restroom. Then we would be called for a couple of one-line quotes. As far as mainstream America was concerned, we should have been named the Public Restroom Advocacy Coalition.

Transgender was barely a social issue, and certainly not a political one. *The New York Times*' coverage of Lobby Day was the first time it or any other major outlet covered trans rights as a legitimate political story (i.e., "hard news").[131] [132] [133]

Even among the LGB-but-not-yet-T media, we were still a fringe issue that was largely ignored. I recall the editor of a major gay newspaper patiently explaining that they wouldn't cover the violent murder of Brandon Teena in Falls City, NB because *he wasn't gay or lesbian.*

No national or state-wide gay rights group included transgender people. On the legal front, GenderPAC had sparred with Lambda Legal, the nation's pre-eminent gay legal group, for years over its refusal to take transgender plaintiffs.[134] (Today the Lambda and the ACLU are leading the fight for transgender rights in the federal courts.)[135]

It was homosexuals that were constantly in the crosshairs of the religious right. Transgender was just too off-beat and too small in number to be important politically. The right's two-fold response to our first Lobby Day illustrated of this. A mobile news crew from the Christian Broadcasting Network (CBN) set up at our press conference in front of the Capitol to ask a single question: Were we advocating for transsexuals to teach grade school children? Then they packed up and left. The next day, Concerned Women of America ran a cartoon caricature of hirsute actor Jamie Farr as crossdressing Cpl. Maxwell Q. Klinger from the TV show *M*A*S*H* answering the phones in a Congressional office wearing a dress and make-up.[136]

Tellingly, CWA's attack was aimed at cross-dressers; it didn't even *occur* to them to attack transsexuals. CBN's response was the more prescient of the two. Along with *gays in the military*, the idea of "avowed" homosexual teachers recruiting them for their "deviant lifestyle" had created a major panic on the right. Just three years later, an FRC director would explain that "Gaining access to children has been a long-term goal of the homosexual movement." Even today, this canard of homosexual "grooming" remains the staple charge of the right. Transsexual teachers were not even a topic, but apparently unfamiliar enough with transgender people, CBN simply repurposed their gay attack lines, because what they really cared about was the specter of *homosexuality.*

CBN's use of childhood innocence and vulnerability were integral to the rights' decades of attacks on gays. As scholar Lee Edelman explains in *No Future*, it is The Child's procreative potential that guarantees the survival of the heterosexual nuclear family, and all the social hierarchies that depend upon it. The homosexual was positioned as a kind of predatory "folk devil," who always threatened to groom and then seduce The Child, ruining their God-given procreative potential.[137]

Simply substitute *gender* for *sexuality*, and *parent* for *homosexual*, and you have the rhetorical framework the evangelical Christian right would reuse in launching its moral panic against the gender-affirming parent: The

Child is innocent and vulnerable, the affirming parent a predatory "folk-devil," one who grooms and then seduces their child into the evils of *transgenderism,* which ruins them for marriage and heterosexual procreation.

But that's today: back then, GenderPAC would have welcomed being attacked by any other rightwing group, because it at least would have acknowledged our existence. But we seemed forever anchored to the margins of the national consciousness. And this was crippling a group attempting to be seen as the new edge of civil rights.

I remember thinking often that one day, transgender people would be part of the national dialog, and—just like women's or gays rights before them—transgender people's rights would be seen as a valid civil rights issue.

Today, nearly a quarter of a century later, transgender is finally front and center on the national agenda every day. Just not in the way sane person could ever want.

This book is *that* story.

Chapter 2 — From Gay to Transgender

In retrospect it was perhaps inevitable that the fight over trans rights would lead back to bathrooms, which were originally the focus of its anti-gay attacks. Restrooms are the only space where we must be intimate with others in public: eventually we all find ourselves in the same cramped unventilated space performing our most private bodily functions next to complete strangers. And because women and girls must bare their entire genital areas to relieve themselves, women's bathrooms can seem particularly vulnerable spaces.

All this has made the public restroom the perfect site for igniting regular moral and racial panics in the right's endless battle against racial, women's, and gay equality advances over nearly two centuries.

With the advent of the Industrial Age, women increasingly began working in factories and mills. It was believed that when the Fairer Sex went outside the home, alone and unescorted, they needed a "Separate Sphere" for their safety. Governments stepped in to create this new sphere, and Massachusetts mandated the first sex-segregated public bathrooms in 1887. And by 1920, all but three of the 48 states had followed suit.

Soon other public spaces—such as libraries or public waiting rooms—had their sex-segregated spaces as well.[138] [139] And these quickly became the center of another rightwing crusade: maintaining segregation-era Jim Crow. Racists portrayed Black men as sexual predators, seeking to prey on white women, and Black women as carriers of diseases that spread via toilets or sinks. In 1961, Memphis used widespread public fears of venereal diseases to justify its refusal to desegregate public library restrooms. In 1966, the first Black college student to be murdered in the struggle for civil rights was 21-year-old Sammy Younge, Jr. of the Student Non-Violent Coordinating Committee (SNCC), shot by a white gas station attendant for trying to desegregate a Tuskegee AL gas station restroom.[140] [141]

By the 1950s and 60s, the emerging "homophile" rights movement brought new awareness to the existence of homosexuality.[142] The right used this to ignite a round of a moral panic over *homosexuality,* based on the canard that gay men were lurking in public toilets so they could seduce young men into lives of depravity. This was accompanied by regular public service announcements of the dangers of public restrooms, police dragnets that targeted consensual same-sex adult activities, and main-stream media promoting highly sensationalizing reporting. An unintended classic of this latter genre was CBS Reports' 1967 documentary, *The Homosexuals.* Actually quite progressive for its time, it opened with anchor (and later *60 Minutes* host) Mike Wallace ominously intoning:[143]

> *"The average homosexual, if there be such, is promiscuous. He is not interested or capable of a lasting relationship like that of a heterosexual*

marriage. His sex life, his love life, consists of a series of one-chance encounters at the clubs and bars he inhabits. And even on the streets of the city —the pick-up, the one-night stand, these are characteristics of the homosexual relationship."

And then there was women's rights. Rightwing hysteria about bathrooms reached a grotesque apogee in its defeat of the Equal Rights Amendment (ERA), which passed Congress in 1972 with overwhelming bipartisan majorities (354-24 in the House, and 84-8 in the Senate).

The ERA was sent to the states for final ratification, and two years later just five states remained of the three-quarters needed. Desperate to roll back women's equality, white evangelical fundamentalist Phyllis Schlafly and her partners rebranded the ERA as a unisex bathroom bill, that would force women to stand in restrooms side-by-side with men and exposing them to sexual predators. Schlafly also claimed that the ERA would lead to legalizing gay marriage and turned her Eagle Forum on gay rights—even after her son John came out as gay.[144] [145] [146] Ex- Governor of California and soon-to-be President Ronald Reagan claimed the ERA would "degrade and defeminize women, by forcing them to mingle with men in close, intimate quarters." Schlafly and Reagan had enunciated the identical political frame that would be repurposed for anti-trans bathroom bills half a century later.

The public restroom—which had only recently been filled with predatory Black men looking to attack white women, and then with predatory gay men looking to attack young boys—was now filled with predatory straight men looking to attack young women. It was a crowded place.

Since the remaining states were all Southern, Schlafly drew on the anti-segregation language of Jim Crow, claiming that the ERA would "integrate public toilets." One anti-ERA flier made the racism even more explicit: "Do you want the sexes fully integrated like the races?"[147] This was a racist dog whistle that no Southern legislator could miss, and few could afford to overlook. On June 30, 1982 the ERA passed the deadline for adoption, falling just three states short of ratification.

But the right's sustained attacks on homosexuals unanticipated a side-effect effect: helping turbocharge the new "homophile rights" movement and introducing the public—even if an entirely retrograde way—to the existence of gays, lesbian, and bisexual Americans all around them, and with decades of organizing and investing, 50 years later it would all finally bear fruit.

In 2003 "sodomy" was still illegal in many states, especially across the South, and almost solely enforced against gays. But on March, 2003, in *Lawrence v. Texas,* the Supreme Court invalidated all of them, finding that adults had a right to engage in consensual private sex. Making matters worse, the Court was led by arch-conservative Nixon appointee William Rehnquist, and dominated by seven Republican-appointed justices. It was a huge setback, one that infuriated white evangelical Christian nationalists who accused the Court of inventing a *right to anal sodomy* in the Constitution.

According to Gallup, as recently as 2001, a majority of Americans still disapproved of gay people by a robust 53% to 40%. Even by 2009, the public was still evenly split, 49% to 47%. By an inflection point was coming, and with it public opinion would begin a slow, irreversible U-turn that only accelerated with time.[148] Just five years later in 2014, a yawning 20% gap had opened up, with the public approving by 58% to 38%, and this would soar to 71% to 25% by 2022—a shocking 46-point gap.[149] It was a huge victory. Yet it was also this overwhelming approval of gays that led directly to the evangelical right's decision to targets transsexual and transgender Americans.

A similar, if delayed U-turn happened with gay marriage. In 1999, the public still disapproved of marriage equality by almost two-to-one, (62% to 35%). Even a decade later in 2009, things had improved but it still disapproved by a robust 57% to 40%.

Yet by 2014, more of the public approved than disapproved—and by 2022 a whopping three-quarters approved of gay marriage (71% to 28%).[150] The Supreme Court's *Obergefell v. Hodges* decision the following June of 2015 legalizing gay marriage arguably followed, rather than led, public opinion. That it was delivered once again by a Republican-dominated Court, with the majority opinion written by Reagan-appointee Anthony Kennedy who provided the crucial fifth vote, only rubbed salt into wounds already raw from *Lawrence v Texas.*

And then, almost exactly five years to the day after *Obergefell*, in 2020 a Supreme Court dominated by arch-conservatives—including two Christian extremists (Gorsuch and Kavanaugh) who had just been appointed by Trump to overturn abortion rights—ruled in *Bostock v Clayton* that LGBT people were protected from discrimination under the 1964 Civil Rights Act.[151] [152]

Bostock's 6-3 majority opinion was not even close. The majority opinion written, by Trump's first Supreme Court appointee—far right Justice Neil Gorsuch—was joined by arch-conservative Chief Justice John Roberts.

If the *Lawrence* legalizing of sodomy, and then *Obergefell's* legalizing of gay marriage had begun closing the door to the right's war on gay people, *Bostock* nailed it shut. Gays were now a normal part of society: three Supreme Courts—each all dominated by far right Republican-appointed judges—had just said so. Seventy years of anti-gay culture wars were officially over.

Wounded and vindictive, an infuriated evangelical right began searching for new vulnerabilities it could exploit to claw back momentum and reignite the war. And the elephant in that room would be transgender people, specifically transsexuals and others who wanted to change their sex or gender.

Even many gay people still had trouble accepting transsexuals. A substantial minority of the gay community saw gay and transgender as two separate communities and issues.

In fact, it just in 2014 that the President of the Human Rights Campaign (HRC), the nation's largest gay rights group and the last national LGB-only hold-out, addressed the largest annual transgender conference and committed the organization to full transgender inclusion,

This inclusion had long been the strategic goal of transgender advocates during two decades of activism. At the time, the total budget for national transgender rights groups was probably less than five million, while the budget for national LGB rights groups was fast approaching $100m. We had always known that the best chance to gain civil rights was beneath the umbrella of the larger LGBT movement.

But transinclusion was still controversial. Just six years earlier, HRC's previous president had addressed that same conference and made the same promise of full transgender inclusion—only to perform an embarrassing about-face when HRC's board revolted. You could almost hear them thinking: *"These 'trannies' are going to just kill us with middle America."*

At the time, many of us in trans rights were contemptuous of what we considered weak-kneed, *real politik* thinking. But as events would show, they had a point—although it wasn't the one they thought. Adding transgender people didn't slow down gay rights in any meaningful way. But the great political leverage and access that being part of the larger LGBT movement meant that we were no longer that small, marginal social fringe that the right couldn't be bothered to attack. On the contrary, we were now the biggest vulnerability of the new "LGBT" movement. That was the hidden price of inclusion. As an APP disinformation report hyperbolically titled *Transgender Leviathan* would note accurately, "the sheer immensity of the 'transgender leviathan' is unprecedented relative to the size of the group it claims to represent."[153]

Evangelical Christian nationalists, infuriated by two decades of defeats in the court of public opinion and its own carefully-curated Supreme Court was going to make trans people the poster child in the new backlash they were creating for the post-*Lawrence*, post-*Obergefell,* post-*Bostock* world. As the ACLU's Strangio put it, the War on Trans youth was "very much a response to the Obergefell decision…This fixation on trans people was because the Christian right needed somewhere to go after they lost marriage equality."[154] The tail was now wagging the dog.

But while trans people might have attracted the full attention of evangelical extremists, the public still didn't know us all that well. A 2016 Pew survey would find that 87% adults knew someone gay, but just 30% knew someone who was transgender.[155] This rose to 44% by 2022. A similar survey around the same time by the Trevor Project would find just 29%.[156] [157]

Whatever the exact number, it was low and significantly less than those who knew someone who was gay. The public may have accepted gays and lesbians, but its attitudes toward trans people were still unformed, undereducated, and often ambivalent. And with trans-sexuality—and particularly the specifics of gender-affirming medicine—there was not just unfamiliarity but profound discomfort. And this was for transsexual *adults.*

Lack of information, ambivalence, discomfort: these were ideal soil for the right to seed a new moral panic, and rightwing extremists began to shift the culture war from sexual orientation to gender identity—or more simply, from sexuality to gender. Millions of dollars that had been devoted to attacking *homosexuals* were now repurposed to studying transgender people's social vulnerabilities, developing effective smears that would exploit public fears, and creating political strategy. And by the end of 2019, they would strike back with a vengeance.

The fact that transgender issues were still a political vulnerability should have surprised exactly no one. The rise of modern gay rights was based on a strategy of erasing the topic of gender nonconformity from public discussion of gayness. One no longer mentioned effeminacy among gay men or masculinity among lesbians in polite company, and the subject was gradually erased from gay rights discourse as outdated, and possibly even homophobic.

As theorist David Valentine explains, this gender-mainstreaming of gay rights promoted a very neat system in which *Gay=Sexuality* and *Trans=Gender*. Henceforth, gayness no longer had anything to do with gender, and any discussion of it by gay advocates was carefully confined to transgender people.[158] Henceforth, gayness was solely about middleclass ideals of romance, equality, and family ("Love Is Love").

This was an immensely successful strategy in making gayness more palatable to middle America (as three successive Supreme Court decisions had just shown). Gay people were no longer "just like" straight people—gay people *were* straight people.

Unfortunately, erasing the topic of gender queerness among gays and lesbians created this immense overhang between the public's knowledge of gender nonconformity and movement's new embrace of transgender people, who were now the last really *queer* thing left about being LGBT. Drag queens and "Dykes on Bikes" might proudly lead annual Gay Pride Parades every summer, but they were then conveniently disappeared the other 364 days before they became a political liability. Unfortunately, this meant *we* were now that liability.[159]

But this strategy of foregrounding gay normativity while pushing gender nonconformity onto trans people, which had worked so well and for so long, was about to come to an end. And this would be especially true with what would turn out to be the most explosive aspect of the coming war on transgender: trans children. Because however little the public might know about the medical specifics of "changing sexes," it knew even less when it came to providing it to young people.

It wasn't until 2007 that pioneering endocrinologist Norman Spack opened the first pediatric gender clinic at Boston Children's Hospital. Even most gay rights advocates knew relatively little about the subject, and the movement was totally unprepared for the ferocity of that attack on trans kids that was coming.

And the coming War on Trans youth would be both qualitatively and quantitatively different from past righting attacks around homosexuality or women's rights. First, the latter had both attacked adults; this was the evangelical extremists' first attempt to demonize children.[160]

And second, both of latter targeted tens of millions of adults. But the moral panic around transgender targeted a truly miniscule portion of the population, a minority within a minority within a minority that totaled a few thousand kids each year at most. To put it in some context, about 500 anti-transgender bills were introduced in 2022—that's about one for every two teens who got top surgery that year. Put another way, in 2022 there were about 3,700 Republican state legislators in the states— that about one Republican legislator for every transgender child who started affirming medical.[161 162 163]

Yet somehow the evangelical right would take this handful of struggling adolescents and transmogrify them up virtually overnight into a huge threat to the nation's social fabric. It was akin to the Great Masturbation Panic of the 19th century in which upper-classes in England and America became obsessed with the fear that their children were destroying their procreative potential (not to mention risking life-long insanity).[164]

Whole communities organized to protect themselves from their own children: tightly tying their hands to bedposts at night, inspecting their underclothes during the day lest they become *too tight*, and closely supervising once-harmless playground activities like sliding down a pole or climbing a tree which were now understood to be as morally dangerous.

An entire layer of society turned its panicked attention to the peril posed by the onanistic child: this once-innocent creature that it had suddenly and alarmingly discovered. which now posed a threat to its very survival, and which had to be contained and controlled at all costs.[165]

Just so, beginning in 2019 white evangelicals across the U.S. suddenly began obsessing over the "danger" posed by the tiny population of transgender kids they had just discovered living in their midst, and the urgent need for massive legislative retaliation that would strictly limit and regulate the *damage* they could do.

It points to one of the stranger facets of the fundamentalist evangelical mindset, which is its tendency towards a paranoid and backward-looking view of life in which any deviation from white Protestant male hetero-sexuality is deviant and dangerous, and the only way forward is always to return to the distant past ("Make America Great Again"), Thus, social progress by women, gays, and now transgender people are always threatening Our Way of Life.[166]

Unfortunately, it is the nature of human societies to progress. If you equate social change with immorality and spiritual degeneration, you are going to feel aggrieved and victimized most of the time ("This American carnage stops right here….".[167] [168]).

Thus, according to evangelical Christian nationalists, trans people and *gender ideology* are leading America over a cliff of moral decline, including(as APP founder Robert P. George has written) wife swapping, polygamy, group sex, prostitution, man-on-dog bestiality, and *both* brother-sister *and* parent-child incest—but also pre-marital sex, out-of-wedlock birth, divorce, contraception, abortion, sex-change surgeries, pornography, and pedophilia. It will be, in the immortal words of Dr. Peter Venkman from *Ghostbuster*—"An epic disaster of Biblical proportions: Human sacrifice! Mass hysteria! Dogs and cats, living together!"[169] [170]

It is telling that almost this entire *parade of horribles* centers on just three problems: sex, sex, and sex. As theorist Michel Foucault observed, Judeo-Christian cultures have proposed procreative sex as *the* central question of morality and social stability. This is why APP's Schilling would reportedly tweet that Russia and China were "behind the American sexual revolution because they knew it would weaken us and eventually destroy us."[171] It is also why autocrats across the globe—include Vladimir Putin in Russia, Viktor Orbán in Hungary, Jair Bolsonaro in Brazil, and Recep Erdoğan ("lesbians, schmezbians") in Turkey have all attacked so-called "gender ideology" in posturing as pious defenders of the traditional family values from encroaching Western moral degeneration.[172] [173]

In 2022, even President Putin extended his sympathies to the writer J. K. Rowling her being attacked by transgender activists because of her repeated and outrageous transphobia.[174] I want to pause here for a moment, because this some trajectory: in 1995, we couldn't buy a mention in the public debate. Three decades later, struggling after a disastrous start to the first European land war in 70+ years, the President of Russia tries to rally his war-weary nation by…attacking transgender people? It was head-snapping.[175]

Attacks like these resonate particularly well where people are politically-conservative, racially intolerant, aggressively religious, and sympathetic to violent authoritarianism: the very qualities that characterize white evangelical Christian nationalists here. A Southern Poverty Law Center found that nearly two-thirds (63%) of Republicans think that transgender people "are trying to indoctrinate children into their lifestyle," and almost four-in-10 believe that trans people are an active threat to children.[176]

So, at first glance, adult transgender people—and particularly transsexual women—would seem to be the natural target starting for reigniting an anti-gay culture war. But as the right at last began to reckon with the bitter reality that its war on homosexuality was over, it quickly realized that it could also simply pivot to attacking transsexuals.[177] North Carolina was proof of that. In fact, it was impossible to understand the crusade against trans children that evangelical Christian nationalists unleashed and the feverish response it elicited across half the nation without first understanding what happened in North Carolina.

Chapter 3 — A False Dawn

2014 May

A wave of state "bathroom bills" which sought to demonize transgender adults as objects of fear and menace had already been introduced in Arizona, Florida, Kentucky, Minnesota, Missouri, and Texas, but none passed. And most were just attempts to pre-empt local non-discrimination ordinances in states' liberal cities. But they were still signs that a rightwing backlash was building.

Then in May 2014, Houston passed the fortuitously named HERO act (Houston Equal Rights Ordinance). It was a perfectly ordinary local ordinance, modeled after existing federal legislation, and prohibiting discrimination based on the usual list of factors such as sex, race, religion, disability, and sexual orientation or gender identity. It easily passed the City Council by 11 to six.

Even in ultra-conservative Texas, such bills were neither new nor remarkable. Fort Worth (2000) Dallas (2002), and Austin (2004) had passed similar ordinances and El Paso, Brownsville, and Arlington offered the same protections through policies and other statutory means. None had generated any pushback or attention.

Nonetheless, Houston's evangelical community sprung into action, collecting signatures for a referendum that would rescind HERO. It was rejected by the City Council because it lacked the necessary number of signatures and because many of the signatures collected were clearly fraudulent.[178] The case when to trial and the local court, which reviewed all the evidence firsthand, agreed and upheld the Council's rejection.

Despite this, on appeal, the far-right Texas Supreme Court returned the referendum to the upcoming November 2015 ballot, ruling with inescapable logic that—although the signatures were fraudulent— the city was obliged to honor them anyway. As Slate pointed out, it was "more a policy statement than a legal ruling... resuscitating the campaign against an equal rights ordinance that the Court clearly didn't like."[179]

Even so, the anti-HERO referendum was given slim chances of passage since polls showing that voters supported HERO by 45% to 36%. Houston was hardly an anti-LGBTQ+ hotbed, and six years before had elected Annise Parker, the first openly lesbian mayor of any major city. And then it reelected her two more times. In fact, on her way out of office. Parker would even throw her public support behind HERO.

But the evangelical right—channeling the ghost of Phyllis Schlafly—did what it always does when confronted with social progress: it launched a panic over bathrooms. Rebranding HERO as "the Bathroom Ordinance," it loudly claimed that HERO would allow male predators to dress up in women's clothing so they could invade women's rooms and assault women.

Lt. Gov. Dan Patrick explained with complete inaccuracy, "The voters clearly understand that this proposition was never about equality—that is already the law. It was about allowing men to enter women's restrooms and locker rooms...."[180] T*he Texas Tribune* reported that "outside of polling places, signs read 'NO Men in Women's Bathrooms,' And television ads depicted a young girl being followed into a bathroom stall where she was cornered by a mysterious older man...."[181]

2015 November

There had been no reports of a crime wave of men dressed in in high-heels and skirts, assaulting women in cities like Fort Worth, Dallas, Austin, El Paso, Brownsville, and Arlington, most of which have had the same protections for over a decade. But no matter: it worked, just like it always works. In November, Houston soundly rescinded HERO by the lopsided margin of 61% to 39%.

That June, in Gloucester County, VA on the Chesapeake Bay north of Newport News, high school student Gavin Grimm had come out as transgender. The Gloucester County is about 90% white, and over two-thirds white Christian.[182] According to the ACLU (which represented Grimm), the Gloucester County School Board responded by "adopting a discriminatory new policy prohibiting boys and girls 'with gender identity issues'" from using the correct restrooms.[183]

Even after Grimm "began receiving hormone therapy (which altered his bone and muscle structure, deepened his voice, and caused him to grow facial hair), [and] obtained a Virginia state I.D. card listing his sex as male, underwent chest reconstruction surgery, obtained a court order legally changing his sex to male under Virginia law, and received a new Virginia birth certificate reflecting that his sex is male," the Board refused to relent. In fact, even after Grimm's graduation, the Board still refused to provide him with a school transcript that he could use to apply to college that matched his male sex.[184]

ADF offered to represent Gloucester County *pro bono* in their Grimm lawsuit. The County was not alone: ADF reportedly sent emails to school districts all over the country, encouraging them to adopt its model anti-trans policy, and offering to represent them *pro bono* if they were sued for discrimination.[185]

In fact, in almost every facet of the coming War on Trans youth, ADF, along with APP will be a prime mover.

ADF was founded in 1994 as a Christian legal nonprofit dedicated to "restoring the Body of Christ" through use of the legal system. It began by providing model legislation for anti-gay marriage bills in Colorado, Idaho, and South Carolina. With record revenues in 2021 of $104.5m budget of over $50m, scores of full-time staff attorneys, and an international network of thousands of "allied attorneys active in 100 countries worldwide," ADF is perhaps the wealthiest far-right hate group, the largest anti-gay group (it has promoted both anti-gay conversion therapy and criminalizing gay sex), and certainly the largest Christian nationalist legal firm in the world.[186] [187] [188] [189] According to the ACLU's Gillian Branstetter, ADF also apparently authored every anti-transgender bill passed by states in 2022.[190]

ADF's single largest funder appears to be the Servant Christian Foundation, which has reportedly donated $50m to its work.[191] Among its major donors is billionaire David Green, founder of Hobby Lobby, which claims to *honor the Lord by operating according to Biblical principles* and famously won a Supreme Court case allowing it to discriminate against its female employees' reproductive health needs because of its corporate beliefs.[192 193 194]

Green is also reportedly a key funder behind Kentucky's Creation Museum (in which humans and dinosaurs cavort together in 4,000 B.C.), DC's Museum of the Bible (which was discovered to have faked its renowned collection of Dead Sea Scrolls), and the aforementioned PR campaign to rebrand Jesus Himself as a Savior who "gets us"—although presumably not the "us" who are queer.[195 196 197 198]

2016 Feb.-March

HERO, *Gloucester v Grimm,* and similar battles attracted a lot of publicity, but there had still never really been a successful attack on the trans community as a whole. But North Carolina changed that.

It started out innocuously in February 2016, when Charlotte—the state's largest city— passed a routine HERO-like measure which added sexual orientation and gender identity to its existing nondiscrimination ordinance. Of course, one byproduct was that it would allow trans people to use the correct bathroom. A similar effort had failed one year before, but this one passed and was set to take effect in just two months.

The state legislature wasn't even set to convene until that May, but sensing a true civic emergency—or perhaps just an opportunity for an easy political slam-dunk—the required three-fifths of the state's representatives voted to call themselves back into session early.

HB 2 preempted all local city non-discrimination ordinances and immediately passed the House. Then just three hours later—with 11 Democrats walking out in protest—it also passed the Senate. Then that same evening, Gov. Pat McCrory signed the bill into law.[199]

It had taken just 11 hours from start to finish—no doubt a record for any North Carolina legislation.

Rightwing extremists have tended to be very deliberate in picking their culture war issues and strategies. Think tanks develop bogus justifications and publish disinformation, legal groups draft model legislation, media groups refine message platforms with outrageous lies through polls and focus groups, and so on.

But HB 2 came and went so quickly that it was unlikely that any of this had occurred. It was a truly spontaneous outburst of legislative zeal. And in the coming transgender battle over sports and then affirming care, the right would not make the same mistake again.

At the time, polling on the HB 2 was all over the place, with surveys from Gallup and Pew showing North Carolinians split on the issue. But the human cost was immediately apparent: over the next 24 hours, calls to the state's TransLifeline suicide hotline doubled.[200]

Back in Charlotte, "Mayor Pat" McCrory had been a popular, pro-business Republican for 14 years. But once installed in Raleigh as governor, he was surrounded by its MAGA-style Republican super-majority and quickly became a far-right culture warrior. When student Gavin Grimm came out, he fulminated publicly over "deviants" invading women's restrooms, directing Atty. Gen. Roy

Cooper—his presumed Democratic opponent in the upcoming election—to ensure that North Carolina's schools never had to suffer the humiliation of being "forced to open sex-specific locker rooms and bathrooms to individuals of the opposite biological sex."[201]

"Mayor Pat" was now using language lifted directly from ADF literature. As the *Washington Post* summarized: "and just like that, North Carolina became ground zero for the heated battle over… transgender rights."[202]

But the backlash to HB 2 was brutal, immediate, nationwide, and without precedent, surprising everyone on both sides. It went far beyond the usual politicians and civil rights groups, engaging an incredibly broad range of American society:

- Major corporations, including Deutsche Bank and PayPal, announced they were halting long-planned, multi-million dollar expansions, and 80 corporations signed an open letter condemning HB 2;
- The States of California, Connecticut, Minnesota, New York, Vermont, Washington, and DC and three dozen cities (from Atlanta, Portland and LA to conservative Cincinnati) banned government employees from non-essential travel to North Carolina;
- Conferences, conventions and trade shows by the dozens cancelled their events, (including at least one police conference); and,
- Media outlets including Lionsgate's Hulu, Turner Broadcasting, A&E, and 21st Century Fox all announced they were cancelling or reviewing plans to film shows and movies in the state.

Ironically, many of the cancelled events and investments had been planned for Charlotte, the state's largest city and home of the original trans-inclusive ordinance.

But bad as all this was, worse was still in store. Major sports joined in. The NFL, ESPN, and NASCAR all announced they were reviewing plans to hold any future events in the state.[203]

The NBA went even further, announcing that upcoming annual All-Star Game— an event which attracted huge national audiences and would bring in millions in state revenue—was being moved from Charlotte, home of the NBA Hornets.

Finally, in a state where college basketball and football teams are practically state religion, with devoted followings among exactly the kind of conservative white males to which the red meat of HB 2 had just been thrown, the National Collegiate Athletic Association (NCAA) announced it was stripping North Carolina of all hosting rights for *seven* of its upcoming major tournaments and championships.[204]

Even prominent athletes and entertainers began speaking out. Michael Jordan, owner of the Hornets and a former North Carolina Tar Heel, came out against HB 2. Performers like Bruce Springsteen, Demi Lovato, Itzhak Perlman, and Maroon 5 all cancelled performances, as did Ringo Star formerly of the Beatles.

The Boss AND The Beatles? His Airness? NASCAR? It was really pretty breathtaking. But these were the forces coming together to take a nationwide stand in favor of transgender people's rights to use the bathroom.

Back in North Carolina, McCrory tried to hang tough, making all the expected noises of state defiance. But the handwriting was on the wall.

By the end of March, an AP analysis found that the building economic boycott would cost the state nearly $4 billion, and McCrory and his allies began looking for an exit.[205] They couldn't know it yet, but there wasn't one: there was only surrender.

But first, they would try a couple tactical retreats before giving in to the inevitable.

2016 April

On April 12, less than three weeks after his triumphant signing ceremony for HB 2, McCrory issued Executive Order 93 which allowed private companies to set their own transgender non-discrimination policies in regard to bathrooms, showers, and co-ed facilities. This fig leaf did nothing to change the law and even less to stem the tide of businesses streaming from North Carolina into the open arms of competing states.

Next a pseudo-compromise was brokered whereby Charlotte would first repeal its anti-discrimination law, and then state—its *casus belli* gone—would repeal its HB 2. But this fig leaf didn't cover much more than the first, and the details were quickly lost in the back and forth as city and state legislators argued over who would do what for whom first.

2016 May

Then on May 9, Attorney General Loretta Lynch, the first Black woman to head the DOJ *and* a native of North

Carolina,[206] announced that the US Department of Justice was filing suit against North Carolina. But what was even more remarkable was the unusually emotional and forceful language she used for what are always pro-forma announcements.

First, Lynch directly cited the battle against racist Jim Crow laws, explicitly placing the struggle for transgender rights in the context of the long struggle for Black civil rights (not exactly an uncontroversial position). Then, just as her statement seemed to be winding down, Lynch turned to the camera and—in an extraordinary and personal statement—declared, "Let me speak directly to the transgender community itself. Know this…We see you. We stand with you. And we will do everything we can to protect you."

It was stunning. I'm embarrassed to admit that this actually gave me shivers watching it. In fact, just writing those words now it *still does*.

And I was not alone. A *Washington Post* headline the next day read "How Loretta Lynch's Speech Brought Some Transgender Advocates to Tears:"

> *There are a few—and only a few—moments in*
> *U.S. political speech-making that LGBT rights*
> *activists recall as particularly seminal for their*
> *cause [where] they have heard the government*
> *come to their defense so unequivocally and so*
> *eloquently.*[207]

When Lynch finished, I turned to my wife of 16 years and my 10-year-old daughter who were also watching, and said emotionally, "Well, we're finally normal." This was the same daughter who had asked a few years earlier in second grade if she could call me "Daddy" when we dropped her off at school, because classmates kept taunting her by asking, "Who was that guy in the skirt?"

It was this moment, and not Lavern Cox's lovely May 2014 *Time* magazine cover, which was the *real* "Transgender Tipping Point."

A business-as-usual law mandating state-sponsored discrimination against transgender people had been passed and corporations, sports teams, organizations, and entertainers along with the federal government had risen up in opposition.

Four days later, on May 13, Obama—who barely five years earlier had announced himself still "evolving" on the issue of gay marriage—directed the Departments of Justice and Education to issue a joint statement declaring that all public schools must allow transgender students to use the correct bathrooms, participate in the correct school sports, change school ID; and be protected from bullying.[208] [209]

It was an impressive endorsement of transgender students' rights, hovering mostly between common sense and common courtesy. Nonetheless, McCrory denounced it immediately, and he was joined by a number of red-state Attorneys General who decried it in the harshest terms: *wreaking havoc, insulting and intolerable, blackmail,* and *putting all our children in jeopardy.*[210] Less than two weeks, 21 state AGs sued the Obama administration to block the new federal policy.[211] [212] All of them are among the same states which five years later lead the attacks on school sports and affirming care for youth.[213] [214]

Even with all this pressure, McCrory and the legislature still refuse to cave. But finally, a power greater than the federal courts, than the NBA, than the DOJ *and* the President of the United States all combined stepped in.

2017 March

The NCAA had had enough.

After waiting for almost exactly a year through all of McCrory's half-hearted attempts to backpedal and the state legislature's foot-dragging, on March 23 the NCAA announced that North Carolina would be stripped of hosting *any* collegiate championship in *any* sport until HB 2 was repealed. Amazingly, this still did not prompt North Carolina to decisive action. So, one week later, right in the middle of the 64-team men's and women's national collegiate basketball championships—an annual obsession accurately nicknamed "March Madness"—the NCAA issued…a deadline. It gave North Carolina just 48 hours to repeal HB 2, or else.

In a state which was then home to three major league teams (NBA Hornets, NFL Panthers, NHL Hurricanes), the college teams like UNC's Tar Heels, Wake Forest's Deacons, NC State's Wolfpack, and of course Duke's Blue Devils also had huge, passionate, life-long followings. In basketball, hating "the Dookies" was practically a national pastime, right up there with hating the Damn Yankees. All of these were especially beloved among well-heeled white alumni donors, who showered their alma maters with donations each year and showed up without fail for every game, home or away.

Moreover, the NCAA controlled not just basketball

and football, but *all* of college sports, including low-profile but still-popular ones like soccer, lacrosse, baseball, rowing, swimming, track, volleyball, and field hockey.

It was now a staring contest. And it was not a fair one.

Just two days later with the deadline about to expire, North Carolina blinked, and agreed to undo HB 2. One of McCrory's last acts as he turned out the lights on his way out after losing office was teeing up the repeal of HB 2. It had been almost exactly a year and a week since passage.[215] Even in defeat, McCrory defended HB 2 as needed to "protect the privacy of children in locker rooms, showers and bathrooms."

To recap: The most powerful college athletic association in the U.S. had forced a sovereign state to back down on a major legislative accomplishment which it had passed with overwhelming support in a session specifically called for that purpose because— although the state could fight the Obama administration *and* the courts *and* major corporations *and* Bruce Springsteen *and* The Beatles—it couldn't fight the state's fanatical college sports fans.

And the issue that brought the entire state to its knees? The only topic that ever got GenderPAC any attention for transgender rights: bathrooms. A better writer could to sum all that up, but even after all these years, I can't.

2017 April

A month afterward, on April 19th a three-judge panel of the U.S. Fourth Circuit Court of Appeals ruled in favor of

Gavin Grimm, finding that he was entitled to use the boys' restroom under Title IX of the 1964 Civil Rights Act.

HB 2 was not at issue. But North Carolina fell under the jurisdiction of the Fourth Circuit Court, so the writing was on that wall. ADF and the Gloucester County School Board appealed to the full court to hear the case *en banc*, but it declined.

Then a wild card: the Supreme Court accepted the case for review. But perhaps fearing an adverse decision, the Trump administration withdrew Obama's support for Grimm's case, and the Court reversed its decision to hear it. The ACLU noted that it is "the third time in recent years that the Supreme Court has allowed appeals court decisions in support of transgender students to stand."[216] A total of five federal appellate courts have also ruled either against discriminatory bathroom policies, or else held that bathroom use does not infringe on anyone's privacy rights.[217]

In 2023, the Supreme Court would also refuse to hear an emergency appeal of a stay of West Virginia's bathroom bill, by 7-2.[218] It is one of the biggest wildcards in the War on Trans youth that no one knows how the Court will rule on any of these matters, including affirming care bans.

Six years after his 2015 lawsuit, Gloucester County finally settled with Grimm and the ACLU for $1.3m.[219]

McCrory went on to lose his reelection bid to the Democrat Cooper, who as his AG had not only announced he wouldn't defend HB 2 in court, but had campaigned vigorously against both it and McCrory.[220]

An HRC exit poll found that 57% of voters pointed to HB 2 as their top reason for voting against McCrory.

No North Carolina governor had lost the incumbency in 167 years, not since 1850 when Charles Manly lost over his support for the anti-slavery Compromise of 1850 (which coincidentally put Texas on the path to statehood).[221]

One of Cooper's first acts once he was sworn in was signing the repeal of HB 2. The transgender bathroom wars were over.

Oxford, AL, a small-town hour east of Birmingham, had the honor of passing the U.S.'s last bathroom bill in April 2016, just as McCrory was trying to backpedal one more time. It contained a particularly nasty provision which criminalized bathroom use with a penalty of up to six months behind bars, which was a first. Oxford's mayor justified it as necessary "to protect our women and children."

All of this had been precipitated by Target Stores, which announced the week before that customers and employees were welcome to use "the restroom or fitting room facility that corresponds with their gender identity." Oxford's own Target was just 10 minutes from the city center, off the main drag, I-20, in between Sam's Club, Cracker Barrell, and Chick-fil-A. But a week later, Oxford finally read the room, and the bill was recalled.

There would still be anti-trans bathroom bills introduced in state legislatures—Missouri in 2017, Indiana in 2021, and Oklahoma in 2022—but all of them would die in committee, fail to pass both houses, or mysteriously miss key legislative deadlines. The effort was sputtering to a close. But not before Texas would give it one last try.

In January 2017, Lt. Gov. Dan Patrick lead a

bathroom bill effort, using ADF's model language. It anyone who encountered a trans student in their restroom to sue for $2,000 for their "mental anguish."[222] Another version would have penalized transgender adults with a year in jail and a $4,000 fine. As often happens when rightwing ideologues wander into progressive civil rights discourse, Patrick would get the words right but the meaning hideously wrong. Piously intoning in support of his bill without even a shred of irony, "As Martin Luther King said, 'Our lives begin to end the day we become silent on things that matter.'"[223]

His bill sailed through the Senate but stalled in the House, where it was bottled up by Speaker Joe Straus, an ally of Gov. Greg Abbot. Straus reportedly explained afterwards: "I'm disgusted by all this. Tell the lieutenant governor I don't want the suicide of a single Texan on my hands."[224] As events will soon show, it was not a concern that would trouble Texas Lt. Gov. Patrick, nor A.G. Ken Paxton, nor Gov. Greg Abbott. But Straus was right, and Texas children would try to commit suicide in the wake of their own legislators' actions.

The close of the bathroom wars was a shocking humiliation for the anti-trans Christian evangelical right. It was a sign of the success of the transgender movement's strategy of reintegrating itself back within the larger gay rights movement.

HRC crowed that the repeal of HB 2 and the defeat of McCrory was a "watershed," adding: "when it comes to LGBTQ+ equality, hearts and minds remain forever changed and, on our side… Barely 10 years ago, Republicans—and some Democrats—running for governor were campaigning their support for state bans on marriage equality. But today, as McCrory has proven to the nation, promoting anti-LGBTQ+ discrimination will cost you an election. There is no doubt that Americans have moved inexorably in the direction of equality and have no appetite for hatred from their elected officials."[225]

At the time, not only bathroom access, but the battle over transgender rights now seemed over, definitively so. Who could stand against the President, the NCAA, and the Beatles? Two decades after the 1995 founding of GenderPAC as the first national gender rights organization, trans rights had finally won.

But it was a false dawn. Just over the horizon, a darkness was gathering that would engulf trans rights in half the country only three years later.

Chapter 4 — Legislative Capture

The HB 2, Gloucester County's, and a half dozen similar efforts in locales from Texas to Alabama were signs which no Republican politician with a finger in the wind would miss.

Polling at the time—like HRC's exit survey—seemed to tell a different story. That same May of 2016, CNN/ORC found the public broadly supportive of transgender rights. Seventy-five percent favored laws protecting trans people from employment discrimination, and that included a *majority* of Republicans. And by almost six-in-10, the public opposed to anti-trans bathroom laws, 57% to 38% and Republicans themselves were evenly split on the issue. So, efforts to ignite another bathroom panic were not going to work.[226]

Encouragingly, the 75% who supported employment discrimination protection for trans people was only slightly less than the 80% who supported them for gays, lesbians, and bisexuals—still more evidence that trans rights' strategy of sheltering under the larger LGBTQ+ umbrella was working as long planned.

But Lynch and Obama's days in office were numbered, and in only five weeks left they would be replaced by Trump and AG Sen. Jefferson Beauregard Sessions of Alabama. A changing of the guard was taking place across the government and across the country, and the new regime would sink much lower in its attacks on transgender than North Carolina had ever considered.

Despite McCrory's culture warrior makeover, when he tried to mount a political comeback, Trump would dismiss him as not "standing for our values:" He was trounced by a Trump-backed candidate by 34%.[227] McCrory had recently been a rising star, a darling of the party after becoming North Carolina's first GOP gove-rnor in two decades. Now at age 65, suddenly his political career was over.[228]

It was a mirror image of what was occurring across the U.S. from 2010-2022, as a historically high number of Republicans incumbents were defeated—almost all from districts dominated by enraged white evangelical nationalist based which threw its support behind MAGA insurgents.[229]

It's hard to remember now, but since the Civil War, conservative white racists across the Solid South were *Yellow Dog Democrats* ("I'd vote for a yellow dog before I'd vote for any Republican."[230]) But with the 1964 Civil Rights Act, Democrats that became the party of Black civil rights, and rural white Christian voters began leaving the party in droves. Nixon's "Southern Strategy" in the early 1970s maximized this trend, adding to the Repub-licans' traditional base of business interests and far-right crackpots like the John Birch Society, gathering all the prejudices together into a single party—everyone who was anti-Black, anti-civil rights, anti-immigrant, anti-gay, anti-feminist, anti-abortion, anti-gun control, anti-science, and generally anti-secular society.[231]

All the nuts in one basket would prove to be a

powerful coalition. Republicans used the dog-whistle language of *law and order*, *family values*, and *real Americans*, which avoided overt racism but which white evangelical Christian voters could recognize as their own.

In 1992, Democrats represented 92 majority-white congressional districts located in red states. But three decades later, as the GOP's center of gravity began its long slide from the Northeastern states and their dense urban cores to the sparse rural counties and towns of the South and West, only 19 of these would be left. Trump's shocking election was simply the capstone to a trend that had been underway since the 1960s and shifted into insane overdrive with the election of the nation's first "Muslim" Black president.[232]

From a voting standpoint, combining all the racists and crazies in one party worked beyond anyone expectations. But once in office, GOP politicians reverted to form and focused on their one and only true love: massive tax cuts for the rich and business. leaving the white evangelical Christian base hanging.[233] But that base was now too big to ignore, and in Trump it had at last found a true champion who gloried in attacking everything they hated: women, immigrants, people of color, Muslims, NATO, intellectuals, vaccines, urban elites— anything and everything that excited their sense of grievance and victimization, including queers, especially transgender people.

Because although polling showed that attitudes had improved, they had not budged among the one demographic that mattered: white evangelical Christians.

As the only major pollsters focused on the intersection of religion and politics, PRRI breaks its surveys out by religious affiliation and it polls during the pivotal years of 2019 to 2022 are especially useful in illustrating the underlying dynamics of what might at first appear to be a the "spontaneous" outburst of anti-transgender animosity.[234]

A PRRI poll in 2021 found that just 21% of white evangelical Christians were comfortable knowing someone transgender.[235] The following year, PRRI found that white evangelicals were also the only religious group in which a majority felt that transgender acceptance had 'gone too far' and nearly three quarters felt acceptance had moved too quickly.[236 237 238]

Moreover, in the years after mainstream of society had rallying against HB 2, white evangelical support for anti-trans bathroom bills *more than doubled* to 87%.[239] A doubling of *any* public opinion over just six years is very unusual.[240] It is a sign that while the both country and Christians as a whole are becoming more tolerant of transgender people, more comfortable knowing them, and more supportive of their civil rights, white evangelicals don't know trans people, don't feel comfortable with them, and remain deeply hostile to their civil rights. Indeed, they are virtually the only major segment of society actually moving *backwards* on trans issues.

And their position is unlikely to improve any time soon. Almost two-thirds of evangelicals (60%) say that their views of transgender people are rooted in their religious faith, and that they are living in the End Times of The Rapture, when Christians living and dead will ascend to meet Christ in the air while all the unbelievers will be killed.[241 242 243 244 245] So, this hate isn't going to break: on the contrary.

As a group, white evangelicals have now become a distinct outlier. And the coming battle over transgender kids will not be a normal political fight, but a religious crusade to impose what are essentially its own outlier theological views.

While white evangelicals have been steadily declining as a group, they still comprise 33% of Republicans, and even more importantly fully 40% of voters in Republican primaries, where they turn out in disproportionate numbers.[246] [247] And because their political views are grounded in a common set of religious beliefs, they consistently vote in a more uniform fashion, forming a true "voting block" that no rightwing politician can ignore, or hope to win without.

This is the critical dynamic in red states, where Republicans often have no viable Democrat opposition and so no pressure from the left to moderate their views. For them, the only real election is in the GOP primary, where their biggest political problem is avoiding being challenged from the right as a RINO (Republican In Name Only) and losing the base. So, there is no political downside for virulent anti-transgender posturing, only upside. Those who are hurt weren't going to vote Republican anyway. And the few primary voters who are actually repelled by their antics aren't about to vote for the Democrat opponent over transgender rights.[248]

The net effect of this is that in the 22 states which are Republican-dominated, the politicians who create the laws for transgender people are decided in GOP primaries, where outdoing one another in anti-trans bigotry has no downside and often pays big dividends.

In effect, in the coming War on Trans youth about

one-sixth of the electorate—the only demographic that believes trans rights has happened too quickly, that acceptance of trans people has already gone too far, that still doesn't know a transgender person and wouldn't be comfortable if they did—*that* demographic is now driving the bus on transgender law and public policy in nearly half the country.

This is why there is such an "inexplicable" flood of bills virtually overnight. There is nothing spontaneous about this war. It does not "come out of nowhere." All that has changed is that white evangelical Christian nationalists have redirected the 50 years of firepower and animus for queers that used to be devoted to attacking *homosexuality* and refocused it on transgender.

It's a textbook example of *legislative capture,* in which an interest group grabs control of the legislative process and advances its own interests at the cost of the public's.[249]

In 2021, as Texas legislators vied to outdo each other in introducing the most draconian anti-trans measures, PPRI found that 66% of Texans were comfortable with a transgender co-worker, 61% with a transgender friend and church-member, and 57% with an elementary school teacher.[250]

In deep-red Kentucky, where APP piloted and refined the new War on Trans youth (more on that in a moment), a 2023 Mason-Dixon poll found that 71% were against anti-care bills—*including 62% of Republicans.*[251] Incoming Gov. Andy Beshear vetoed *both* the sports bill and anti-care bills and—in a state Trump crushed by 26%—became one of the most popular governors in the nation.[252] [253] [254] But then, as a Democrat, Beshear didn't have to face the state's white evangelical base in a Republican primary. (Even though nearly three-quarters of voters agreed with the vetoes, the legislature still overrode *both*, the anti-care one in a secret Republicans-only session convened without warning during lunch with the chamber's microphones kept off).[255] [256] [257]

White evangelical Christian nationalists and their bottomless animus towards trans people are the *why* of ACLU's Chase Strangio's observation that this backlash had gone incredibly far and fast in ways that were "completely unfathomable just three or four years ago."

They are the *why* of Erin Reed's time travel to 2019, when just three years ago names and birth certificates were freely changed, transkids played sports at schools, and thousands of dysphoric adolescents were receiving affirming care in all 50 states, and how this world has become unrecognizable.

Because what we didn't realize was that behind the Obama administration's public embrace, the nationwide repudiation of North Carolina's state-sponsored discrimination, and all the positive poll numbers, that all of these were for transgender *adults*.

And what the extremist right realized is that if transgender was the Achilles heel of the LGBTQ+ movement, then children were the Achilles' heel of the transgender movement. As leaked chats from one UK anti-trans group advised it troops succinctly: *focus relentlessly on under 25.*[258] There is virtually no wider understanding or awareness of young people's gender transitions in the dozen or so years since Spack opened the first pediatric clinic. Their right to their affirming medical care is not recognized in law or policy, has not been talked about much, and is something for which gay or trans rights groups have not prepared the public.

There are three national groups with a substantial focus on trans youth: GLSEN—which combats school bullying; PFLAG—which provides supports families of queer kids; and the Trevor Project—which combats teen suicide. There is no group is devoted to trans kids' rights, especially their right to medical care and no group whose mission is promoting the lives and issues of transgender kids. Nor are doctors in a position to do so. So, no one is doing the vital and overdue work of public education about the realities of adolescent gender dysphoria and gender transitions. As so often happens, young people had outrun their own movement.[259]

It was that overhang again between public's knowledge of gender nonconformity and the movement's embrace of transgender. And well-funded extremist evangelical hate groups were about to fill this knowledge gap with disinformation lies…and then panic.

Chapter 5 — How to Attack Trans Kids

For half a century, rightwing attacks on the LGBTQ+ community had focused on gay men as *deviant* and *promiscuous*. But beginning with Anita Bryant's successful 1977 campaign to repeal a Miami anti-discrimination law, the right refocused its attacks from adult immorality to predation on children. In Bryant's case that meant throwing gas on the vile canard that teachers who were openly homosexual would seduce their students. Apparently unaware of the basic facts of reproduction, Bryant would helpfully explain that, "Homosexuals don't reproduce, so they must recruit," and she called her campaign "Save Our Children."

By the 1980s the religious right had adopted children as the centerpiece for its attacks on gay rights. But there was no playbook for how to incite a moral panic about *transgender* children.

Evangelical hate groups needed the HOW.

And according to the Southern Poverty Law Center, that would emerge at a panel discussion on how to attack transgender kids hosted by the Family Research Council at its annual Values Voter Summit. The October 2017 Summit was convened just held 10 months after a man brandishing an assault rifle entered DC's Comet Pizza after the far-right became convinced that prominent Democrats were operating a pedophile ring from its basement (Comet doesn't have a basement), and just two months after the mass Unite the Right march of neo-fascists, white Christian nationalist, and paramilitaries in Charlotte, N.C. at which a woman was killed. Still more signs that a massive backlash is building and just waiting for the right spark.[260] [261]

SPLC's quote below accurately presages the strategies that the right deployed in its attacks on sports and then on medical care. It also shows their awareness of their bizarre new alliance with left-wing TERFs and feminists like Martina Navratilova and J. K. Rowling, who were eager to make common cause with hate groups in attacking transgender children.[262]

Perhaps it was no coincidence that these tactics would come from an evangelical activist engaged in battles over local school boards, where kids are always the issue [*emphasis added; edited for length – ED.*].[263]

Meg Kilgannon, a parent and director of Concerned Parents and Educators of Fairfax County… offered three strategic *"non-negotiables"* in fighting policies on gender identity.

The first non-negotiable was; "Focus on gender identity to divide and conquer.

"For all of its recent success, the LGBT alliance is actually fragile, and the transactivists need the gay rights movement to help legitimize them. Gender identity on its own is just a bridge too far. If you separate the T from the alphabet soup, we'll have more success."

Kilgannon said Americans are not ready to give teenagers gender reassignment surgery or put children on puberty-blocking hormones that may have serious long-term health risks, comparing the practice to "the 1950s lobotomy fad in psychiatry."

Her second non-negotiable: "No personal attacks on LGBT people or parents of transchildren."

Personal attacks, she warned, can be counter-productive. "If you attack trans people, you become the proof they rely on for demanding protection. So don't play into their victim narrative because in this culture war, they are the bullies, not the victims...."

Her non-negotiable: "Don't use religious arguments, because they aren't effective."

Kilgannon said secular arguments can reach a more diverse audience... "[I]ncluding feminists who argue that gender identity is the 'ultimate misogyny' and 'erasure of women.'" She said lesbians are concerned that "transing [sic] masculine girls is a form of lesbian eugenics." Citing shared opposition to gender identity, pornography and prostitution, she quipped, "I had no idea we agreed on so much...."[264]]

She could have added a fourth tactic—When going negative, keep it positive. This final piece of advice was spelled out in an unsigned 2022 Substack blog post from Parents with Inconvenient Truths about Trans (PITT).

Titled, "It's Strategy People," it instructed rightwing activists how to fool major media into carrying disinformation and lies about trans kids, comparing the unpleasant necessity of using positive language when dealing with mainstream media with the necessity of having to use German when dealing with Nazis.[265]

We are being told that we can't use the words "transgender" or the word "gender" at all. [But] we have put parents' faces on two national TV networks, telling the world what's really going on. There's no way this would have happened if the producers had seen words like "deluded" or "mentally ill" on the banner of our website....

[Our approach is working. We have had stories placed in other parts of the mainstream media, like the BBC, Telegraph and Times. Already this year we have had the New York Times, of all newspapers, start to question pediatric transition.... This has resulted in stopping actual kids from being socially transitioned, in actual schools. We successfully got a British de-transitioner on national television. You think that language like "mutilated" will get a detransitioned person on television... Please show me an example of how you did that....

War is about strategy.... Imagine that you are in Nazi occupied France. You're in the resistance, and you need to blow up the railway lines, in order to stop the enemy from advancing. If you don't have a German speaking diplomat on your team, you don't know which railway lines to bomb....

So now white Christian nationalists had their HOW. Next they needed the WHAT—some bogus but scary-sounding issue that would spark the base's outrage. And in November 2019, a year before the presidential election, APP conducted an extensive pilot campaign whose sole purpose was finding exactly that.

Founded in 2009, to re-energize the flagging culture war against "the sexual left," APP bills itself without irony as *the NRA for* families.[266] In other words, its mission is attacking exploiting exactly the kind of political liabilities that all those PRRI surveys identified among white evangelical Republican voters. [I reached out to APP for comment on this book, but it did not respond.]

As the *New York Times* documented in a 2019 article titled," A Conservative Push to Make Trans Kids and School Sports the Next Battleground in the Culture War," APP identified Kentucky as the perfect place to test market its vision for a renewed war on LGBTQ+ Americans, because it leaned to the right, hosted one of the few statewide elections held before 2020, and Republican Gov. Matthew Bevin was having trouble shoring up his base.[267]

APP's current messaging transgender people— "mostly dire-sounding warnings about predatory men being allowed into girls' locker rooms and women's restrooms" had been falling flat. "'Look at the bathroom issue,' said [AAP CEO Terry] Schilling. 'It is the weakest ground we can fight on — on this slate of issues. And conservatives have been fighting on that almost solely over the last several years.'… Added Frank Cannon, the group's founding president. 'The world hasn't fallen apart' since these kinds of laws have failed to pass.'"

In fact, despite introducing dozens of bills from Texas to Alaska that would ban bathroom use as well as birth certificate changes and local non-discrimination laws, nothing had gained traction with voters—including Republican voters—and many had failed to pass.

More importantly, every effort to date had shown no capacity to reignite the kind of outraged moral panic that would jump-start the Christian rights' endless culture war over gender roles, sexual orientation, and gay marriage. If anything, the country had grown more tolerant on trans issues.

A survey by PRRI early that that same year found that more than six in 10 Americans said they were *more* supportive of transgender rights than just five years ago. Although it added ominously, "'Conservative Republicans (40%) stand out as the only ideological group with less than half reporting increased support for transgender rights.'"

And that was the entry point. APP's polling showed that while messages about bathrooms barely moved the needle towards Bevin, a misleading ad showing a boy wrestler as a transgender girl competing against cisgender girls did. And the shift was strongest among voters over 65.

Noted the *New York Times*, APP "is limiting its work to Kentucky for now, but strategists say it has bigger ambitions. It is effectively running a pilot program for the 2020 election that will help it determine how it could use the debate over transgender rights to rally conservative voters in support of President Trump.

The results could inform what type of campaigns social conservatives run in the future — and answer whether the delicate and deeply personal questions around gender identity are the next major wedge issue in American politics or, as recent experience suggests, something that most voters and politicians would rather not see politicized...Said Schilling, 'What we're doing is trying to show Republicans how to win on these key issues.'"

APP's president Schilling later explained to the *New York Times* that they had no particular issue with sports *per se*, it was just that their pilot showed that was "where the consensus was."[268] [269] And he also admitted that the animus towards transgender people had surprised them.

Translation: APP didn't even care about the transgender people they were about to spend tens of millions of dollars demonizing: they were just collateral damage it its attempt to find any weapon it could seize up to rekindle outrage against LGBTQ+ people.

Polling and focus groups probably revealed to APP what the rest of us realized too late: the public's acceptance of transgender rights has limits, and one of them is where cispeople believe that they have lost something that trans people have gained at their expose.

Nobody cared if a transperson someone used the empty bathroom stall next to them. But as Schilling bragged, claiming that cisgender children were being hurt was much stronger because it made it so that transkids were taking something away from them—and that's what got voters roused up. He would later add, "When [McCrory] lost, they basically collected a scalp to use him as an example of what happens to you when you do a bathroom bill. And that was really tough. But that all changed once the transgender sports issue hit the scene."[270]

Pitting one group against another to stir up anger and fear is a tried-and-true rightwing strategy. White Christian nationalists had claimed that providing gays with anti-discrimination protections was giving them "special rights" at the expense of straight people. And attacks on affirmative action continue to focus on claims that people of color are getting jobs and opportunities at the expense of white people.

APP and ADF and their allies are hoping that school

sports (really girls' sports) will help post-North Carolina Republicans get comfortable attacking transgender people again. And once that ball was rolling again, they can expand their attacks to banning medical care—which means effectively banning transgender among kids. And that's exactly what happened.

The problem for Christian nationalist hate groups is that more than three million girls play high school sports, only a tiny fraction of 1% are transgender, and within that that tiny fraction there had been exactly zero reports of Trans Uber-Athletes trouncing the competition and taking over their sports.

But somehow, that made no difference. The claim that transgirls were a "threat" to other girls was a compelling lie. In 2022, when Ohio introduced its "Save Women's Sports Act," the Ohio High School Athletic Association noted that it would affect just one transgender student out of 400,000 young women and girls playing in grades seven through 12. Nonetheless, the Act mandated full genital examinations for any girl athlete "accused" of being transgender. As 18-year-old softball player Ember Zelch told ABC News, "I was the only trans high school female athlete approved to play at that time, so it just felt very much like a personal attack."

Nonetheless, the Republican sponsor, state Rep. Jena Powell hysterically declared that the state's "female athletes are losing championships, scholarship opportunities, medals, education and training opportunities and more to… biological males in girls' sports."[271] [272] [273] (To be fair, the following year that influx of trans athletes that Powell feared did indeed materialize, with their number skyrocketing by 200%…to three.)

So Christian nationalist hate groups had the HOW and the WHAT. But they were still missing the WHO: a single, high-profile case—"the exception that proves the rule"—on which to hang all the lies and fearmongering.

This is harder than it sounds. To begin with, there was that paucity of transgirls actual playing school sports. But even if they could find the one case of a successfully trans high school athlete, it couldn't be in sports like soccer, basketball, or field hockey, where individual effort gets lost in the ebb-and-flow of team effort. It would have to be an individual sport, like wrestling or swimming, where girls go head-to-head. And it couldn't be in elementary school, where sports were mostly just play; it would have to be in high school, where sports are more seriously about competition.

At the time, there was only one trans women in high school who was winning anything in a competitive individual—an obscure runner in Connecticut. But she would be enough.[274]

Chapter 6 — "Saving" Women's Sports

Terry Miller had not particularly been a standout athlete when she competed in boys' track. But after she transitioned, she blossomed, and eventually went on to win state titles and finally a New England girls' championship.[275]

So ADF now has its WHO—the one outlier it needs. As attorney Shannon Minter of the National Center for Lesbian Rights would note, Miller "was their Exhibit A. And there was no Exhibit B—absolutely none."[276]

ADF would now ruthlessly exploit one girl's modest regional success in a nationwide campaign of rightwing hate and vituperation. It didn't hurt that Miller was Black. White America has a long and dismal history of viewing African-American women as lacking the sort of *proper femininity* it associates only with upper-class, Caucasian, Euro-centric womanhood. Or as research Jules Gill-Peterson put it: "It is impossible not to read the lawsuit [against Miller] in light of the long history of anti-Black iconography framing Black girls as improperly feminine, if not masculine, cast as threatening to the purity and innocence of white girlhood."[277]

As Miller would declare to ESPN, "I have known two things for most of my life: I am a girl and I love to run. There is no shortage of discrimination that I face as a young Black woman who is transgender."[278] It is no accident that some of the rights' media ads will feature the largest, strongest-looking, unsmiling transathlete possible, and often one who is of color as well, contrasted against a cheerful, long-haired, conventionally-feminine white girl whose body (although she is supposedly an athlete as well) never shows the slightest sign of muscular development.

ESPN's coverage paints a picture of Miller, her running mate Andraya Yearwood (also transgender), and three cisgender athletes who are among their state's best at what they do, dueling against one another at different distances across different events, again and again.[279]

"If there is a genesis of the legal battle among Connecticut runners, it might have come at the 2019 outdoor State Open. It was there—14 days before the ADF filed its complaint and eight months before it filed its lawsuit against the CIAC—that Smith, Miller, Mitchell and Yearwood all settled into their blocks for the 100-meter final. It would be the only time these four were ever on the track together..."

But the meet was not the first time Mitchell had raced against Miller and Yearwood. She had finished in third place to their first and second places at 100-meters in the 2018 outdoor State Open, and then fourth to their first and second at 55 meters in the indoor 2019 State Open.

Once the race begins, Mitchell shoots out of the blocks and finishes in first place. It a personal-best time of 11.67 and Mitchell's her first state championship. Smith places third ahead of Yearwood in fourth.

But the battle among the runners resumes at the outdoor New England championship just four days later, where Mitchell wins the 100-meter, Miller the 200-meter and Smith the 400-meter.

After Yearwood was outed as trans by the *Hartford Courant*, there had been surprisingly little national notice of her or of Miller, and Yearwood had assumed that it would only diminish. "'If anything, it got worse. I've faced retaliation from people in my state for the past four years. It's just tiring to go through one punch after another…'

"Back in the Floyd Little Athletic Center in New Haven, Mitchell and Miller line up next to each other in the center lanes for their next race. Mitchell had never beaten Miller [and] the 2020 55-meters comes down to these two. The gun sounds, and Mitchell and Miller barrel down the track, arms and legs in unison, stride for stride, before crossing at what looks to be the same time. Mitchell, convinced she crossed first, pulls up as quickly as she can. She trots back toward the finish line, looking up at the screen above the rolled up bleachers to see the results.

"The lights flash. First place, Chelsea Mitchell, 7.18. Second place, Terry Miller, 7.20. For the first time all afternoon, the crowd explodes in cheers and whistles, as Miller silently walks off the track toward her coaches. Mitchell puts her hands on her cheeks in disbelief, beaming."

In June 2019, ADF's files a formal complaint with the Department of Education on behalf of the three cisgender runners: Chelsea Mitchell, Selina Soule, and Alanna Smith[280] Mitchell reportedly complains to the media, "No matter how hard you work, you don't have a fair shot at victory."

Of course, she left out the inconvenient fact that immediately afterwards, Mitchell went on to beat Miller handily in two races over the next nine days.[281]

In February 2020, ADF files a federal lawsuit against Miller and Yearwood, backed by Trump DOE Secretary Betsy DeVos and U.S. Attorney General William Barr.[282] The DOE files a 45-page letter in support of ADF with the Connecticut Interscholastic Athletic Conference (CIAC), and the DOJ files its own letter of support. For good measure, DeVos threatens the CIAC with the loss of all federal funding if they don't pull out of the Connecticut State Athletic Conference.[283]

To the uninitiated eye, it might look like a coordinated effort from the highest levels to magnify a non-issue into full-blown a national panic.

Despite all the rhetoric, ADF is still missing one huge detail: any actual harm its plaintiffs have suffered. None of them have missed scholarships or been denied academic opportunities. They just didn't win a few high school track races.[284] The federal judge hearing the case is unable to find any harms either, and quickly dismisses their lawsuit. ADF immediately appeals, but the 2nd Circuit Court similar finds itself "unpersuaded... that Plaintiffs established an injury" for which judicial relief could be granted.[285]

This may look like a defeat. But ADF is just getting started. Blocked in the courts, they simply turn to their allies in red state legislatures. The court losses are not the point. ADF has established the beach-head for attacking transgender youth, they now have the DOE *and* the DOJ behind them, and they have successfully ignited a huge public debate over the bodies of transgender girls.

You might as well have fired a starting gun.

The first bill out of the gate to be enacted into law is sponsors by Idaho Falls Rep. Barbara Ehardt, who played Division One basketball for Idaho State, coached women's basketball in California and Washington, and finally returned to run a kids' sports camp.[286] It doesn't hurt that 66% of her constituents are white Christians.[287] Even before HB 500 is introduced, Ehardt admits to the Associated Press that she's unaware of a single one of Idaho's 125,000 teens who is transgender and playing school sports.[288] [289]

Ehardt has the perfect Christian extremist credentials. She has previously banned sex-education from schools unless requested by parents in writing.[290] As a Republican colleague explains "'sexual purity' and 'chastity' are still very important…" to Ehardt—presumably meaning for girls rather than boys.

Ehardt has also opposed a bill to end child marriage, because it would have engaged the government.[291] Idaho bears the shame of the nation's second highest rate of married minors, virtually all of them teenage girls married to much older men.[292] This puts on full display the utter illogic of the evangelical Christian nationalist right: child marriage actually *is* a terrible problem for Idaho and affects thousands of its girls yearly, but the government must be kept out of it. Transkids playing sports is a non-problem and affects no one at all, but is a legislative emergency demanding government intervention.[293]

Ehardt also has the right kind of crazy. For instance, she is a leader of the state initiative optimistically called "Greater Idaho" (rather than "Smaller Oregon) which would have 15 counties secede from Oregon and join

Idaho, all because their conservative voters are fed up with liberal Portland, Salem, and Eugene being the three-way tail that wags their rural Republican dog.[294] [295] The whole scheme is reminiscent of the rightwing fever dream of turning the mountainous and remote northwest—90% white and blessed with an astonishing variety of armed and extremist paramilitaries—into an Aryan homeland, literally a nation-within-a-nation.[296] [297] [298] [299]

If ADF and APP had gone venue shopping for just the right place and the person to reignite their LGBTQ+ culture wars, they could hardly have done better.

Although Ehardt would describe herself as "partnering" with ADF, her bill appears to be largely a Xeroxed copy of its. As she explains, "Nobody had legislation like this. No one had anything that would work."[300] HB 500 is stuffed with all sorts of nasty provisions, including that any cisgender girl who has suffered any harm can sue for *monetary damages* for up to two years. In practice, this means a cisgender girl who is traumatized because a transgirl got her out in kickball in fifth grade, or who is upset because a transgirl dunked on her (we can all do this) in junior high, can decide *two years later* to sue for emotional distress…plus attorney's fees.[301]

In addition, it mandates that any child "accused" of being a transgender has to prove their biological sex "as part of a routine sports physical examination relying only on… the student's reproductive anatomy, genetic makeup, or nor-mal endogenously produced testosterone levels."[302] The word "routine" is doing a lot of work here, since submitting to a medical examination of genitalia is not part of *any* school sports exam for girls *or* for boys, and if it was, parents would all pull their kids out of school sports overnight.[303]

In a sign of just how accurate of FRC's Value Voter Summit strategy was of aligning with TERF feminists, the lead signatory on a public letter from a group calling itself "Save Women's Sports" in support of Idaho's new anti-trans bill is... none other than Martina Navratilova.[304]

In a February 2019 op-ed for the *Times of London* one year before, Navratilova had declared that "a man can decide to be female, take hormones if required by whatever sporting organization is concerned, win everything in sight and perhaps earn a small fortune, and then reverse his decision and go back to making babies if he so desires. It's insane and it's cheating."[305] A later tweet would neatly combine rightwing hysteria over men changing sexes to win at women's sports with the longstanding TERF's obsession with male genitalia: "You can't just proclaim yourself a female and be able to compete against women. There must be some standards, and having a penis and competing as a woman would not fit that standard."[306] [307]

Finally, in 2022 she denounces the University of Pennsylvania for nominating transgender swimmer Lia Thomas for the NCAA's Women of the Year, tweeting out: "Not enough fabulous biological women athletes, NCAA?!? What is wrong with you?!!!!!!?"[308] [309] (In response, one writer would note that out of almost half a million total NCAA athletes, according to Outsports only 32 identify as trans, asking rhetorically, "It sounds like you want even fewer transathletes? Fewer than 0.007%?")

The hyperbolic, transphobic name "Save Women's Sports" resonates right back to Anita Bryant's hyperbolic, homophobic "Save Our Children." Navratilova's public support is actually unsurprising, since the HB 500 specifically name-drops her, right up front it in its preamble.[310]

For her unabashed transphobia, Navratilova is applauded by the rabidly anti-gay Family Research Council, citing her commitment to "transcendent truth." FRC neglects to mention that among its own *transcendent truths* is that homosexuals like her are pedophiles who recruit children for sex, and that lesbians are "at war with motherhood, femininity, family, and God."[311] [312] [313]

Just to recap, a one-time trailblazing lesbian professional athlete is now helping lead a nationwide attack by the anti-gay evangelical Christian right on transgender girls who just want to play after-school sports with their friends.

Like every rightwing Christian extremist attacking transgender children, Ehardt will go out of her way to declare that she is not doing so, declaring to the Idaho House that, "I am not trying to exclude trans people from living a full, healthy life." It's the kind of statement that is somewhat reminiscent of white racists passing one law after another to suppress Black voting rights while loudly announcing that they only want to protect *election integrity*.

As ESPN notes, as HB 500 inches closer to becoming law, a 17-year-old cross-country runner named Lindsay Hecox is startled to realize that she alone is the plaintiff for any upcoming lawsuit. "'I said to myself that this applies exactly to me. How many other trans women athletes are in the state of Idaho?'" The entire legislature is bringing its full weight to bear on this one young woman. When HB 500 is signed into law by Gov. Brad Little in March 2020 just one month later, Hecox is still the only transgender high school athlete competing in the state.[314] [315]

After graduation, as her lawsuit is being heard, Hecox graduates and attends Boise State University. Apparently missing the part about her being an athletic superwomen, Hecox fails to make Boise's women's track team, explaining that there were just "too many good female athletes"[316]

The ACLU quickly files to stop HB 500 in court with Hecox as the plaintiff, and the lawsuit is joined by another unnamed plaintiff: a 17-year-old cisgender girl arguing that that having to prove her sex because of her athletic build and "masculine" personal traits is invasive and humiliating. It is one of the first times that a cisgender ally has voluntarily put themselves in the same legal jeopardy as a transgender plaintiff, and it is a smart move by lawyers from ACLU and Legal Voice because it broadens the harms HB 500 inflicts to include cisgender athletes as well.

In August 2020, federal judge David Nye agrees both that "being subject to a sex dispute is itself humiliating..." as well to the more fundamental argument the plaintiffs were "likely to succeed in establishing the Act is unconstitutional as currently written," adding that Idaho "had not identified a legitimate interest served by the Act that the preexisting rules in Idaho did not already address, other than an invalid interest of excluding transgender women and girls from women's sports entirely..."[317]

Idaho has since appealed, and as of this writing, the case is before a three-judge panel of 9th US Court of Appeals.[318]

But as with the loss in the federal courts to Miller and Yearwood, none of this really matters. For ADF and APP, it is a proof-of-concept, which is all they need. That, along with all the national resources they bring to bear, is a complete game-changer. Sports, a complete non-issue for years, is suddenly at the top of the rightwing's target list. As the *New York Times* notes , "Rarely has an issue that so few people encounter… become a political and cultural flash point so quickly."[319]

In 2019, when South Dakota Republicans pushed their anti-trans sports bill, it was given only a number, its two sponsors were both male, and it died quickly and quietly in committee in just 10 days.[320]

In February 2021, when the bill is reintroduced, in place of the simple legislative bill number, the bill has been given a new voter-friendly name: "The Student-Athlete Fairness Act." As one South Dakota ACLU representative notes, "Anytime they give a bill a name in South Dakota, you know something's up." This time its introduction comes with teams of experienced political strategists from groups like APP and ADF, model language from ADF's template; sponsorship by two female legislators; and innocent-sounding messaging honed in focus groups that promote "fairness in women's sports." High-profile supporters are even trucked in from nearly Idaho—which has already passed its own bill—to provide "expert" testimony on the urgency of the problem.[321]

This time the bill's introduction is well-planned and coordinated and it quickly passes. South Dakota has a population of just 800,000, only thousand or so of whom are transgender teens, none of whom have been identified as playing competitive school sports.[322] [323] [324] But since the problem extremists are addressing isn't the existence of transgender teens in sports, it's the existence of transgender teens, none of this matters.[325]

A similar story unfolds in Utah. CNN describes how

when State Rep. Kera Birkeland tried to build support for her anti- trans sports bill, she couldn't get her colleagues attention. Less than two years later her bill has so much support that it not only easily passes the Republican legislature, but when it is vetoed by the Republican governor ("Rarely has so much fear and anger been directed at so few,"), his veto is quickly overridden.[326] [327] According to the ACLU, 20 anti-trans sports bills are filed in 17 states by mid- 2020.

In yet another illustration of the lemming-like behavior that breaks out among rightwing legislators, once they discover red meat issue that riles up the evangelical base, from March 2020 (Idaho) to June 2022 (Louisiana), 19 states pass laws making it illegal for transgender kids not just to compete, but simply to *participate* in any school sport from kindergarten their gender identity, even if it is the gender which they enrolled and attended school and which matches their legal ID, and usually all the way down to kindergarten grade.

2020	Q1	Idaho
2021	Q1	Mississippi, Arkansas, Tennessee, South Dakota
	Q2	Alabama, West Virginia, Montana, Florida
	Q3	Texas
2022	Q1	South Dakota, Iowa, Utah, Oklahoma
	Q2	Kentucky, South Carolina, Louisiana

School sports is a subject unfortunately well-chosen for Republican politicians to be comfortable attacking transgender people again. First, visual knowledge is very compelling, and part of the trans condition is that our bodies often seem to argue against the very things we want to say about ourselves.

Second, many cisgender people are still simply uncomfortable with the specifics of the transgender body, and the coming debate will push them front and center.

Third, it engages the sort of simple slur that can be difficult to unwind. Try to refute the lie that trans people want "to force girls to compete against boys" and you can quickly find yourself mired in discussions about testosterone, sex difference, the true purpose of after-school sports, and so on. And, as they say in politics: *if you're explaining, you're losing.*

Finally, the broad label "school sports" covers everything from Alabama's Crimson Tide multi-million dollar collegiate football system to my daughter playing after-school kickball in second grade. As HRCs Cathryn Oakley put it, "The rules can't be the same for fourth grade kickball as they are for sixth grade JV lacrosse as they are high school track."[328]

But the right's attack successfully conflates all of this, as if every third-grader playing soccer over recess spends her spare moments on the bench deciding between the sponsorship deals her agent has presented from Nike or Adidas. As Strangio explains," [Y]ou're talking about little kids who just want to play rec sports. They just want to get through life."[329]

Or as one exasperated mother of high school field hockey player put it: "[A]ll she really wants to do is sing 'Pitch Perfect' on the bus to out-of-town games, and throw up after she does too many burpees."[330]

But no one is discussing kid-type stuff like socializing, exercise, play or even (God forbid!) *fun.*

Instead, the right *and* the left are enmeshed in an interminable debate about the true degree to which cisgender girls are being victimized, delving into the specifics of the effects of testosterone, pubertal skeletal growth, dimorphic muscular development, and so on. No one ever stops to asks if this is fair to transgender girls (or boys, who will be forced to compete *as* girls); no one centers *their* lives and *their* feelings; in fact, no one speaks to them at all. Everyone is talking *about* them like they're not there. They might as well be potted plants.

Instead of the spontaneous national outpouring against the anti-trans discrimination that occurred in North Carolina, there's a lot of hemming and hawing and foot shuffling and then… silence, as the question of how to deal with the bodies of transgender girls freezes and then silences all the forces that came together so triumphantly just two years earlier. In retrospect, it is maddening to wonder if just a small fraction of the country had done so, if the entire War on Trans youth, which is about to unleash over 1,000 bills across 42 states, would have collapsed like a bad souffle. Because sports is just a trial balloon: the main event is ending care, and that is going to get teed up next.

The evangelical Christian right is testing the country, and the country is failing.

The NCAA, which brought North Carolina to its knees by cancelling all future tournaments in the state in all sports, follows the time-honored tactic of "condemn and move on." It issues a strongly-worded statement, but doesn't even bother threatening to move a couple of early round March Madness basketball games that are scheduled at Idaho's Boise State University.[331] Other major groups and corporations that had spoken out in North Carolina reacted similarly.

It turns out that the public *is* comfortable after all with overt, state-sponsored discrimination against transgender people, so long as it's wrapped in positive messaging and targets only transgender kids. The interregnum, when we thought we had rights, ended up lasting least just three short years.

A March 2021 Gallup poll found that almost two-thirds of the public was suddenly opposed to trans participation in school sports (62% to 34%.) This number included 90% of Republicans—which is to be expected—but also 67% of independent and 45% of Democrats.[332] A June 2022 NPR/Ipsos poll and a *Washington Post*/University of Maryland poll around the same time found similar numbers.[333] [334] [335]

Even in *true blue* California, a 2023 poll would find that twice as many people supported limiting girls' sports to bio-girls.[336]

And almost no one on the progressive left is speaking out in outrage over attacks that pit entire state legislatures against one or two trans schoolkids playing sports.

When even your friends don't have your back, you're really in trouble.

So instead of an outpouring of support, what trans kids get instead is a very public row pitting transphobic lesbian tennis legend Martina Navratilova against trans-positive lesbian soccer legend Megan Rapinoe. I said in the opening chapter that this book would tell the story of how the public came to grapple for first time with the realities of what "changing sexes" really involves. This is what it looks like. And it isn't pretty.

All the pieces are now in place. Evangelical

extremists have the model legislation, the funding, the messaging, the planned disinformation campaign, and the tremendous momentum they've created from attack school sports. Republican politicians, gun-shy after North Carolina over ever attack transgender rights, are now ready for more. The public, which had rallied around transgender people, is divided and ambivalent, as are Democrats and the left.

The next campaign—to end transgender kids' access to medical care and thus the reality of visible transgender kids—will first spark briefly into life in Arkansas, before igniting into a full flame in Texas and then becoming a conflagration that consumes half the country.[337]

All legislative hell is about to break loose. It's going to be open season on transgender youth.

The nation doesn't realize it yet, but a corner has just been turned, and there will be no going back.

Part II
War Begins

Chapter 7 — The Insidious Concern

"This book works to slowly and at length...visit as much destruction as possible upon one central libel that limits the livelihoods of trans children: that they have no history, that they are fundamentally new and... therefore deserving of less than human recognition... I propose an ethical relation that calls upon adults to stop questioning the being of transchildren and affirm instead that there <u>are</u> transchildren, that transchildhood is a happy and desired form—not a new form of life and experience but one richly, beautifully historical and multiple."

--Jules Gill-Peterson,
Histories of the Transgender Child

Rightwing attacks tend to recycle the same reliable villains: the *predatory homosexual*, the *welfare queen,* the *illegal immigrant*, and so on. But paradoxically, in the attack on medical care it will be *parents* who are villains. It is the first minority civil rights struggle in which those under attack are *not* those with the experience of the minority at issue.

The framework will be lifted directly from Anita Bryant's dusty 50-year-old playbook: children as perfect little cisgender heterosexuals who—if they turn out to be gay or transgender—must have been perverted by adults, in this case their own parents.[338] [339]

But how do you demonize loving, caring parents, while appearing not to? The right has a HOW problem again.

The answer is provided in March 2019 by the Heritage Foundation at an obscure and poorly-attended panel that was one of the first presentations by the evangelical Christian right on banning pediatric medical care. Instead of criticism of transgender youth, it featured moving declarations of deep concern for their well-being ("keep it positive…").[340] This wasn't *discriminating:* it was *helping.* A year later, a legislator introducing yet another heartless anti-care bill would describe it as an "act of love," even as terrified parents and their children fled his state.

The same evangelical Christian nationalist organizations, which were obsessed with taking away transgender kids' rights to school sports, are about to pivot a full 180 degrees to pose as their helpers and defenders. It's a tactic that anthropologist Mikey Elster has termed "insidious concern," in which assaults that call for trans people's eradication are paradoxically framed as care and compassion.[341] In sum, the right is going to protect trans children from unintentionally hurting themselves with their own gender identities, much as one might protect an unwitting child from hurting themselves with a sharp knife, or a hot stove.

It was a massive display of the rankest kind of *concern-trolling*—an obvious sop, a bone to throw the public and freeze the left. And what's surprising is that it will work so well.

The panel moderator was the Foundation's Ryan Anderson, reportedly a notorious homophobe whom

GLAAD notes still supports *conversion therapy* to "cure" homosexuality, which he has compared to alcoholism and pedophilia. During the presentation Anderson would weirdly extoll the benefits of just letting transgender "boys who prefer traditionally feminine activities and girls who prefer climbing trees and playing with trucks [to] go on to become generally healthy gay and lesbian people as adults."[342] [343]

What he *doesn't* say is that both he and Heritage allegedly consider "generally healthy" gay and lesbian adults to be pedophiles who seduce children. This head-snapping *up-is-down*, *black-is-white* messaging is as public an admission as possible that the extremist evangelical movement has really moved on from gays rights and is now fully committed to assaults on transgender people.[344]

The presentation itself is saturated with biased science and *faux* concern: "These [suicide] statistics are tragic, and they should stop us in our tracks" and "Transition affirming therapies are virtually untested and inflict lasting harms." It also connects hormonal treatment with brain impairment, cancer, heart attack, monkey pox, blood clots, liver failure, and hypertension as and of course premature death. Apparently gender affirming care is almost as deadly as playing with a loaded-gun. Of course, Heritage never mentions the urgent need to warn all the tens of thousands of parents over the last 50 years who have provided exactly the same hormones to treat their children for *precocious puberty*.

But then, the playing field was rigged against transgender teens in the very way medical care was defined.

Studies show that almost 5,000 teens get breast implants

each year, and about the same number get breast reduction. And attitudes towards this have become so casual that it is increasingly common for teens to even request top surgery as a "graduation present" upon completing high school.[345] [346] [347] [348] Moreover, about 30,000 teens each year also have surgeries to their faces which often "are motivated by body dysphoria, peer pressure, invidious internalized notions about race and ethnicity…[and] social expectations of femininity."[349] [350] According to the American Society of Plastic Surgeons, all told almost a quarter million teens are having some kind of non-medically-necessary procedure annually.[351] And not just teens, pediatricians have quietly been treating thousands of children as young as seven with hormone blockers annually.[352]

But none of these figures has anything to do with transgender youth. Instead, they're all about the hundreds of thousands of cisgender adolescents who ask for and receive a wide variety of affirming medical interventions each year in order to better align their bodies with their sense of gender.

To put this in perspective, 282 trans teens age 13-17 had top surgery in 2021: that just three percent of the nearly 10,000 cisgender teens who got top surgery, and it's only one-tenth of one percent (.12%) of the quarter of a million teen gender affirming surgeries in total.[353] [354]

In other words, trans kids are a rounding error on a rounding error. But this one-tenth of one percent are the ones getting procedures to *change* rather than *reinforce*, their genders. So, each of the dozens of anti-care bills contain specific exemptions for cisgender kids getting exactly the same procedures.[355] And when West Virginia Democrats—citing Republicans' repeatedly cries of such procedures' *"irreversibility* and *life-long impacts"*—try to amend the state's strict anti-care bill so that cisgender breast enlargement and reduction are also banned, Republicans uniformly oppose it without giving any reason.

What this double standard means in practice is any teen in any state can have one or all of the most commonly-requested gender affirming procedures— breast augmentation/reduction, labiaplasty, liposuction, otoplasty (ears), rhinoplasty (nose), even the famed "Brazilian butt lift"—so long as they're *not* doing it to change their gender.

It is a form of what scholar J. R. Latham has called "trans exceptionalism."[356] And the double-standard extends to Intersex Genital Mutilation (IGM), which remains the Standard of Care for "treating" intersex infants, although regret rates among adults are astro-nomical. [357] [358] [359]

The overwhelming majority of these surgeries are not to correct dangerous abnormalities but for the purely cosmetic purpose of making intersex genitals better resemble cisgender ones. Yet *every* state bill introduced to ban trans care includes a specific exemption to ensure that IGM continues uninterrupted, infuriating intersex activists because—unlike trans affirming care—IGM really *is* an "irreversible" and "life-long" alteration inflicted on a non-consenting child.

But red state legislators know next to nothing about intersexuality, and are simply xeroxing an ADF template. When Montana State Sen. John Fuller is questioned during debate about the IGM carve-out in his bill, he is flabbergasted, responding in outrage by de-manding, "How does *that* relate to this bill?"[360] [361]

As legal blogger, Evan Urquhart would note, "There is a sort of tacit cultural agreement to treat treatment for gender dysphoria as something different, outside the normal rules of medicine, that goes largely unexamined and unmentioned."[362] Because of their general unfamiliarity, gender-affirming or "sex-change" procedures are often perceived by the public and the press as a dark, strange corner of medical practice. Nothing could be further from the truth.

Not only have all the procedures long been part of mainstream medical care, but almost all were originally developed for and perfected on cisgender people long before being offered to transgender people. Even bottom surgeries—among the most complex gender affirming procedures—were developed for and perfected on non-trans patients.[363]

But while there is nothing new about affirming care, what is new is how many trans youth have begun requesting it. While still small in absolute terms—a few thousand each year—the number more than doubled from 2017 through 2021, when the right launched its War on Trans youth. (See Appendix B).

Hovering between .1 and .6%, trans identification among the young and old has been relatively stable for decades.[364] [365] By for the generations that have grown up under the combined effects of smartphones, social media, and the huge normalizing impact of the *Obergefell* and *Bostock* decisions, overall LGBTQ+ identification has grown by as much as 630%, and trans identification specifically by as much as a whopping 850%.[366] [367] [368] [369] [370]

Generation	Trans-Identification	
Generation Z	1997 to 2004/2012[371]	1.9%
Millennials	1981 to 1996	1.0%
Generation X	1965 to 1980	0.3%
Baby Boomers	1946 to 1964	0.2%

When Johns Hopkins Hospital opened the first adult gender clinic in 1966, it's head of plastic surgery described his patients as "hysterical," "freakish," and "artificial."[372] Paul McHugh—reportedly a notorious and proudly anti-gay homophobe who had allegedly helped defend numerous pedophile Catholic priests—was eventually brought in to head its department of psychiatry with the express intent of shutting it down, doing so in 1979 after little more than a decade in operation.[373][374]

McHugh would declare that he didn't dislike transsexuals, but considered them sick and wanted to help them get the psychiatric help they needed—introducing the same "insidious concern" rhetorical frame that Heritage would promote for attacking trans kids which the right would broadly adopt four decades later. In fact, Hopkins was probably the first example of white Christian fundamentalists mounting a successful institutional back-lash against affirming care. Of the 20 hospitals that followed Hopkins into the field, all but three followed it in closing their clinics.[375] And this was how controversial medical care was *for adults.*[376][377]

But what emerges in the surveys by Gallup and Pew is a generation of trans *and* cis youth that is comfortable crossing traditional boundaries of sex and gender, and—as demonstrated by the expanding popularity of affirming surgeries, piercings, and tattoos—with embracing a broad variety of body modifications.

Using the historical averages of .1 to .6%, one would expect to find about 58,000 to 350,000 transgender young people in Gen Z. Instead, the total probably is probably more like 1-2m.[378] [379] [380] This is easily large enough to drive social change as they enter adulthood. For comparison, about two percent of the population is Jewish, and about the same two percent is Mormon.[381] [382] As the New York Times notes, youthful trans identification had become "political dynamite."[383]

Among transgender youth specifically, this is an explosion in slow motion. It is what a social tipping point looks like, a true generational shift. And, as with all such shifts, it will create shock waves, and the War on Trans youth is one of them. Because all this is occurring just as white evangelical Christian nationalist hate groups are looking for that first post-*Obergefell* panic they can leverage to reignite 80 years of anti-gay culture wars. And Texas will be their first victory; the ignition for all that comes after, including a full-on assault to eradicate all visible public acknowledgment of the existence of transgender children and youth.

But Texas is too large, complex, and business-oriented to simply pass a bill through its legislature.[384] Instead, the ban on care will ricochet through a large cast of the sort of outsized personalities for which the state is rightly notorious, each adding their own particular flavor of crazy, before finally being enacted through blatantly illegal means.

Among the first is an obscure and strange individual named Jeffrey Younger. In pictures, Younger appears as tall and middle-aged, with thick black glasses, a full beard, and thinning hair. He is a committed conservative

Christian, allegedly a serial liar, and—strangely for someone about to play a central role in the nation's first successful ban on affirming care—has allegedly claimed to be
a homosexual.

It's unclear if Christian nationalist organizations like
ADF and APP were actively searching for a front-man to
launch their new attack on care. But if they were, they had
found him in Jeffery Younger.

Chapter 8 —When Texas Came for Our Kids

If it had not been for Chloe, I could have been one of those people attacking the Capitol on January 6th. That's how my family is. I was an ordained minister at the time, and I spent the better part of a year making her life horrible doing what I thought was right. Chloe was only three or four, but everyone thought the devil was trying to use her for evil. After a year of conversion therapy, she was praying to go to heaven and be with Jesus, so she could be a girl. She would rather go to heaven and be with Jesus and live as herself for eternity, than stay here and live as boy one for more day.

--Kaylee, Parent of a Transgender Child

2010

In 2010, Younger meets a blond-haired Dallas pediatrician named Anne Georgulas, who in pictures often appears to be smiling gently and engagingly, the way you might want your child's doctor to look. Georgulas will later testify that she married Younger in part based on how accomplished he was. According to court papers, Younger told her he was a once-divorced career Marine who had passed up a $250,000 career opportunity to go and fight the ground war in Iraq;, that he had since worked for Fortune 500 companies, regularly earning from $100,000 to $225,000 annually; and that despite all this, he had found the time to earn two degrees from the University of Dallas and then a Ph.D. he had almost completed from the University of North Texas, where he had taught mathematics.

It's a stunning resume. As Georgulas would also testify and the court would later confirm, almost none of it is actually true.

According to court documents Younger has not been divorced once, but twice. He's had no hard-core Marine combat experience in Iraq or anywhere else but had been separated from the Army—not the Marines— after a brief stint "due to an admission of homosex- uality"—which he apparently acknowledged at the time. (A source close to the family alleges that this was a ploy to collect the cash enlistment bonus being offered, but details are murky.) Court records show Younger has never even earned more than $100,000 except for a single year. He not only earned substantially less than claimed, but he has been on unemployment regularly —including at the very time he dated Georgulas and bragged of his financial prowess. He does not have two college degrees, and but zero, has never been a university professor, and there is no record of him ever teaching mathematics to anyone.

In fact, it is fair to ask if Georgulas actually knew the man she reportedly met on the dating website *PlentyOfFish.com* at all when they wed that December. Certainly, she had no idea that she has just married a man who will become the standard bearer for Texas' coming assault on transgender children—including the daughter she is about to bear.

2012

In 2012, two years into their marriage, Georgulas has twins, James and Jude, with eggs she has purchased. By age two, James is already showing an attraction for feminine toys and appearances and is soon imitating the popular female stars from Disney's movie *Frozen* and asking to wear dresses, even announcing at age three: "I'm a girl." By age five she is also asking to be referred to by female pronouns and be called "Luna." By now, Luna, is consistently dressing and presenting as a girl, and eventually enrolls in grade school as a girl as well.

Georgulas is highly supportive, Younger is just as vehemently opposed. A bitter and protracted bitter struggle over the boundaries of Luna's gender expression begins in earnest. Younger is adamant that they will raise their daughter as a boy; Georgulas is equally adamant that they will support their daughter as the gender she is.

2014

In October 2014 in Dallas, pediatric endocrinologist Ximena Lopez opens the GENECIS clinic.[385] From a deeply conservative Hispanic Christian family, Lopez reportedly faces enormous personal misunderstanding and friction because of her commitment to helping transgender children in need. Her medical *bone fides* are impeccable: she has trained at Massachusetts General Hospital/Harvard Medical School under Norman Spack himself.[386] And GENECIS' *bone fides* are hardly less distinguished: it is housed at the Children's Medical Center Dallas and is run jointly with the University of Texas Southwestern Medical Center, both distinguished medical centers.

GENECIS is the first such clinic in Texas, the only one in the southwest, and at the time one of only four in the entire country. According to Lopez, the hospital—which has regularly been taking in depressed and suicidal young transgender patients in its emergency rooms (for whom it has no gender services to offer) strongly supports GENECIS's launch.[387]

Gen Z is coming of age in Texas, and within just a few years, GENECIS will be joined by two more clinics in Houston. This will grow to more than a dozen, including 10 Planned Parenthood Health Centers that provide evaluation, blockers, and hormones.[388]

2015

None of this is under-the-radar. On the contrary, the following June in 2015 the *Dallas Morning News*, the state's second largest paper, carries a 2,000 word-piece on its website under the celebratory headline, "Free to Be Themselves," complete with pictures of smiling transkids and factoids about Dallas' transgender community.[389] [390] There are no howls of outrage, much less a cascade of anti-transgender legislation in Austin, the state capital.

But it is the calm before the storm. Lopez, her clinic, and its young patients are about to become collateral damage in the political bonfire over on transkids' care which will consume the state in just six years, Younger will be holding the matches, and *Georgulas v. Younger*—still just a private annulment hearing in a local court—will provide the key spark.

According to court findings, Younger has begun acting aggressively toward Georgulas' two older daughters from her previous marriage, including withholding possessions, forcing them to do "plank push-ups" as punishment, and even specifying the patio as the site because its pebble surface would be extra painful.

By February 2015, Georgulas has had enough, and asks Younger to move out. Three months later, she files for divorce because of "insupportable discord and conflict of personalities." This initiates the long and painful legal battles common to every contested divorce, where lawyers duel over custody, child support payments, visitation rights, and, of course, blame. But this two-year battle is inflamed by truly irreconcilable differences over little Luna's gender identity.

By October 2015, Georgulas amends her divorce petition to request that their marriage be completely annulled. She also sues Younger for defrauding her of $45,045.11 he had requested to buy a new truck, which it appears he later sold for cash.

Only months later, the Charlotte City Council passes its non-discrimination bill, and North Carolina's battle over transgender bathroom rights about to start.

2016

By the following year, Georgulas' marriage is annulled and she's awarded the $45k for the re-sold truck. With Georgulas' annulment, she and Younger begin the tricky, bruising, back-and-forth dance of shared custody—in their case made nearly impossible by the ongoing and deeply toxic dispute over four-year-old Luna and her gender.

The custody hearing is presided over by Judge Kim Cooks of the 255th Dallas District Court. According to an interview in *Attorney at Law Magazine*, in her spare time Cooks works as a fitness trainer and competes professionally in the Women's Bikini Division of IFBB Bodybuilding contests. It is safe to say with regard to issues of womanhood and femininity, Cooks is not exactly gender nonconforming. She issues "interlocutory orders" that cover such details as visitation schedules, child support, schooling decisions, and so on while the custody trial is pending before a jury. The ILO grants Georgulas and Younger joint custody, but makes no stipulations about how they are to handle their disagreement over Luna's gender.

2018

Younger appeals the annulment and divorce settlement to the Court of Appeals for the Fifth District. In July, 2018 the Court of Appeals upholds Georgulas verdict on both the marriage annulment and the $45k reimbursement.

Reportedly during Younger's custody, he continues to deadname and mispronoun Luna, shaming and intimidating her about her feminine appearance. He is also allegedly bullying her about her hair, which is already short, going so far as to cut it into the "high-n'-tight" Marine-style (something he never does with her twin brother, Jude). At one point he allegedly advises Luna that she should change from playing soccer to rugby because it's "a real man's sport."

Still apparently infuriated about his daughter, Younger launches the online campaign SaveJames.com, complete with smiling pictures of him with Luna as a little boy. To this will eventually be added a SaveJames Facebook page and a fundraiser at the Christian website GiveSendGo, which reportedly raises well over $100,000. While the authorship of the following excepted SaveJames Facebook post is unclear, it still provides a flavor of the proceeding:

> *Hey guys... The word that was given from God to him is this: Anne is being spiritually op-pressed. Pray for her heart and for her to be set free. What is being done to James* [sic] *and Jude is Satanic and evil. Pray for the demonic hold over Anne Georgulas to be broken. THIS WILL BREAK IN JESUS NAME AND HAS BEEN FORETOLD! It will be hard and the fight will become more intense. The devil has been having a field day and James has been targeted as a sacrifice for his agenda.... God be with us all as we continue to fight! —
> Chambers of My Heart*

> *#ChildhoodStolen #LetKidsBeKids #SaveJamesSaveThousandsOfChildren*
>
> *#MedicalChildAbuse #ProtectJamesYounger #SaveJames*

Younger claims that it is Georgulas who is forcing Luna to be a girl against her will, seeking to "chemically castrate" her with hormone blockers, forcing her to undergo "mutilating" surgeries, etc., etc. Also that the judge and the court-assigned counsellor are both against him, and the judge has ordered him to accept Luna as a girl, something he will never do. In one interview, he reportedly brags defiantly, "I'm never going to pay doctors to do any transgender procedures on my son. I'm not going to pay for prescription drugs, I'm not paying for any transgender counseling, and I'm certainly not paying for a transgender surgery," apparently implying that the court is forcing him to do things against his will, according to court records, none of this is true.[391]

A 2019 study from the journal Family Court Review examined 10 mothers who have been "affirming" with trans children who were challenged by their husbands for custody rights. In 100% of these cases, the husband alleged that it was the mother who had *caused* their child to become transgender. (Sadly, in several cases, this tactic was successful and resulted in the judge denying the mother child custody rights.)[392]

The court-assigned counselor, Benjamin Albritton, attended Dallas Theological Seminary ("Our mission is to glorify God [and] build up of the body of Christ") and then at Biola University ("…a biblically centered education"). In other words, he is not exactly a Manhattan liberal and probably could have been hand-picked by Younger himself. Moreover, the court counseling sessions are entirely anodyne, covering such harmless *Parenting 101* topics as Setting Good Boundaries, Noticing Signs of Bullying, and Constructive Conflict Resolution. Albritton is also far from transgender-positive, at one point complaining that by allowing Luna a transgender flag, Georgulas "might have been immersing him [*sic*] in that particular mindset…" In another session Albritton even plays the Fashion Police, advising Georgulas that Luna's wearing a dress and low heels to their session is "a little overdressed [when] your typical girl might wear leggings and sandals…"[393]

Since no one involved in the trial has any background in child development, much less in gender issues, portions of the court sessions can unintentionally read like low comedy. For instance, here's Amicus Stacy Dunlop, a court-assigned lawyer who represents the children's interested at trial:

Dunlop: *So in the backyard she'll whip it out and pee against a tree?*
Georgulas: *Well, there are no trees, but yes.*
Dunlop: *That's kind of boyish, right?*
Georgulas: *I think it's also more convenient…*

At age five puberty is way over the horizon, so Luna has no sex hormones to block. As for "mutilation," no gender-affirming top or bottom surgical procedures are carried out on prepubertal (or even adolescent) children, trans or cis.[394] In fact, since girls and boys are generally pretty much the same physically until puberty except for their genitals, managing such children is entirely social and confined to decisions about style (clothing, hair, jewelry, etc.) and identification (name, pronouns, school records).[395] So none of Younger's claims appear to be true.

What is true is that Younger himself appears clever, highly verbal, and (as the court puts it) a man who "finds comfort in public controversy and attention [by pro-claiming] unfounded facts and is motivated by financial gain…at the cost of the protection and privacy of his children." Younger, a man who invented a macho military combat life he never lived and alpha-male business success he never had, is re-inventing himself again as a kind of avenging angel of the evangelical Christian right, with

119

gender-affirming care as his cause. Expanding his "Save James" campaign, he writes, grants interviews, and knocks on doors in Austin, the state capital, apparently searching for a means to leverage himself and his cause to the next level. To the untrained eye, this might appear to be more of the MAGA grifting so common among the Christian nationalist right, looking for an issue that will generate outrage so that it can be monetized for profit, like a certain Grifter-in-Chief.

Whatever the reason, in, 2017, one of the doors Younger knocks on is that of a wealthy Dallas/Ft. Worth real estate developer and former State Senator, Don Huffines.

Huffines is lean and short with wavy white-hair, apparently fond of appearing in boots and an outsized cowboy hat. He has been a member of the Texas House's ultra-right Freedom Caucus. Needless to say, "freedom" here refers to things like carrying guns and ending property taxes (a favorite for a property developer)—not private decisions about your child's gender or medical care.

Huffines has also been a co-sponsor of Texas' own bathroom bill, which contributed to his losing his Senate seat by 10 points to a Democrat who campaigned against it and Huffines's culture warfare in favor of bread-and-butter issues that Dallas voters cared about. The city is not exactly a fertile ground of hot-bed radical extremism, although in 2004 it elected a Hispanic lesbian, Lupe Valdez, its County Sheriff.

The lesson Huffines apparently takes away from his loss is that it's time to take his show on the road to the entire state, so Younger's timing is unfortunately good. Huffines wants to launch a campaign for governor and needs to take down Abbott to win. Younger (as the court noted) enjoys the "comfort of public controversy and attention for… financial gain."

As *Vox*'s Katelyn Burns explains, the entire country-wide campaign to ban affirming care is about to grow "directly from the social media disinformation campaign surrounding Luna Younger…[and] the bitter custody battle between parents who disagree over her gender identity.[396] Huffines starts attacking Gov. Abbott as soft on the issue of transgender kids.

2019

On October 22, 2019 a jury awards pediatrician Anne Georgulas sole custody of Luna and her siblings by 11-1. The following day, the trial escalates into a state matter. Younger's engaging Huffines finally bears fruit: Abbott tweets out, "FYI the matter of [the 7-year-old child] is being looked into by the Texas Attorney General's Office and the Texas Department of Family and Protective Services. #James Younger"

The hashtag tells it all: hair length, pronouns, and dress of Luna now have the full attention of the Lone Star State.

An anecdote in a lengthy *Texas Monthly* profile is unintentionally revealing about what is about to occur:[397] As State Attorney General, Abbott had established a $1.5m "Special Investigations Unit" to hunt down those engaged in "epidemic" of voter fraud, which naturally found nothing. But it did succeed in harassing, a 69-year-old Black woman from Fort Worth named Gloria Meeks, who had unwittingly helped her elderly, housebound neighbor vote by mail, and during the ensuing investigation, surveillance and harassment by the state, suffered a stroke.[398] [399]

It was an early instance of Abbott's pattern of abusing state power with other would-be autocrats like Trump and DeSantis, who prefer ruling by fiat like mafia dons rather than by law. And this is particularly the case with contentious, high-profile issues like abortion, immigration, voting rights... and now transgender children.[400] There were already 34 lawsuits against Abbott for various Executive Orders pending. And now for the first time, Abbott is about to bring the full weight of a state's power to bear on the gender of a seven-year-old transgender girl.

Apparently at Abbott's request, A.G. Paxton sends a referral letter to Texas Department of Family and Protective Services (DFPS), the state foster care agency, requesting that it investigate Georgulas for possible child abuse for allegedly proposing chemical and surgical treatments to permanently alter Luna's sex—charges Younger has been making repeatedly and publicly. DFPS soon shows up at Georgulas home to investigate her.

With Paxton's letter, the big guns of right wing get involved. Trump Jr. and Cruz tweet about "child abuse;" Ultra-right U.S. Rep. Dan Crenshaw charges that the mother was considering administering hormones blockers to her prepubescent child, and various Texas lawmakers get in on the act. In the midst of this avalanche of political pressure from the highest levels, the very next day Judge Cooks *overrules* her own jury's 11-1 verdict, ruling instead that Georgulas and Younger will be awarded joint custody. She explains that Texas "has no compelling interest...[in] requiring the father to affirm the child and honor the child's choices."

Maybe not, but shortly the state *will* take an

overwhelming interesting in ensuring that the child's choices are *not* affirmed.

As *Vox*'s Katelyn Burn would explain, rightwing outlets would now start driving the conversation about care. In the week following the initial jury decision, 23 conservative news sites published 55 stories about Younger and opposing Luna's transition. According to data from Media Matters, those 55 stories earned 3.5 million Facebook interactions.*"[401]*

With this attack from wing-nut media, Georgulas becomes the target of the virtual mob piles-on so dismally familiar in the age of rightwing firestorms, fed by the accelerant of anonymous social media accounts. She receives death threats and is doxed on Facebook. Her pediatric practice suddenly starts getting highly-negative online reviews by random people, and dead animals are left outside the office door of her practice, which is about to be closed anyway. Finally, the Dallas PD shows up on her doorstep to inform her that they have found credible death threats against her on the dark web, and advise her to close her practice immediately. She does so.

Like so many unwitting parents who populate this book, who had built lives in Texas and themselves became caught up in the right's bottomless appetite for theatrical cruelty, Georgulas now makes plans to leave the state for good. By December 2022, she will leave for California, one of three states which has passed transgender sanctuary laws (and the first to do so specifically for transgender kids and not as an afterthought on an abortion sanctuary bill).[402] [403]

Judge Cooks forcefully pushes back on state lawmakers who have begun charging that Georgulas is surgically or chemical "castrating" Luna, posting her Facebook page that, "No Texas judge or Texas court nor the 255th Family Court or any of its judges has ordered the chemical castration, puberty blockers, hormone blockers or any transgender reassignment surgery on this child to become a female…"

But the mob is already in full howl and for this inoffensive and entirely factual statement, Cooks begins receiving death threats of her own.

Georgulas sues to have Cooks recused for cause and that December, retired district court Judge Tena Callahan agrees with her, removing Cooks.

2020

Inexplicably for a state whose population is roughly that of Greece, Portugal, and Sweden *combined,* and whose quarter *trillion* dollar budget is larger than that of half the member states of the European Union, Texas' state legislature is one of only four that meets every other year.[404] Even then, its legislature is only in regular session for less than six months.

But it is currently out of session during the 2020 national election, which apparently provides a brief pause on new developments. However, there are two major national developments. First, on March 30, back in Idaho Falls, thanks to ADF and Barbara Ehardt, Idaho passes the nation's first state-wide anti-sports bill. Second, on June 15th the Supreme Court issues its landmark *Bostock v Clayton* ruling, banning employment discrimination against LGBTQ+ people.

Shockingly, the ruling is authored by hyper-conservative Justice Neil Gorsuch and is joined by conservative Republican Chief Justice Roberts.[405] *Bostock* enrages the Christian right, feeding the growing fury against LGBTQ+ people, and as 2021 opens, it will relaunch the War on Trans youth a vengeance.

2021 January

A mob of thousands of supporters storm the Capitol Building in DC, apparently powered core groups of white evangelical paramilitaries and allies wielding Christian signs and iconography and claiming to enact God's will to *stop the steal.*[406]

2021 February

The fuse is lit in neighboring Arkansas, home to its own unique political culture. Arkansas is no longer the Land of the Clintons. On the contrary, it has become a haven for the anti-trans, anti-DEI, anti-woke evangelical right. Upon being sworn in as governor in 2023, among Sarah Huckabee Sanders first E.O.'s is banning the use of the new gender-neutral adjective *Latinx.* Arkansans across the state, Anglo *and* Latinx, would breathe sighs of relief.[407]

In February 2021, State Rep Robin Lundstrom, who has been honored for her "Christian Values" by the Bible-oriented Arkansas Family Council, introduces HB 1570 *aka* The "Save Adolescents From Experimentation act. "SAFE" would ban insurance reimbursement or the use of state funds for adolescent gender care, sanction health professionals who provide it, and allow any patient to sue for a medical provider who has provided them care for a minimum of two decades (until they turn age 38).[408] [409]

2021 March

Arkansas's legislature had already overwhelmingly passed an anti-trans sports bill, as well as a bill exempting doctors with religious prejudice from treating LGBTQ+ patients. It then quickly passed HB1570, outlawing medical care for kids, the following month. The bill is vetoed April 5th by Governor Asa Hutchinson, who explains that it interferes "with physicians and parents as they deal with some of the most complex and sensitive matters involving young people [and] denying best medical practice to transgender youth can lead to significant harm…"[410]

This is surprisingly compassionate and common-sense explanation from a Reagan Republican who is governor of a deeply red state. And the fact that he's voicing it at all is due largely to a private 20-minute meeting he held immediately after the bill's passage with pediatric endocrinologist Michele Hutchison, who had come to the state with the encouragement of GENECIS' Ximena Lopez and with the express intent of opening the state's first GAC clinic, Gender Spectrum. When it opened in 2019, Gender Spectrum was is warmly welcomed by the Arkansas Children's Hospital—the state's only pediatric institution—which had little to offer its young transgender patients and families, who had to make the 10-hour round trek from Little Rock to Dallas to get treatment.

According to Michele Hutchison, in its first year, Gender Spectrum would see just a handful of patients. But as news spreads, that trickle grows until its finally becomes a flood: by 2022, 350 families have gone through the clinic's doors. Ironically, in a culture where trans issues are not much publicly discussed, HB 1570's introduction will act like massive infusion of free advertising, virtually tripling Gender Spectrum's intake of young people almost overnight.[411]

Hutchinson had signed an earlier anti-sports bill, yet also demurred that he didn't really see any problem requiring remedy.[412] This mirrors veto statement sports bills by Utah's Cox, Indiana's Eric Holcomb and North Dakota's Doug Burgum, Kentucky's Matt Bevin dismissal of the need for a bathroom bill, arch-ideologue and Trump-wannabee Gov. Kristi Noem trying to both veto South Dakota's sport bills while also keeping it at least partially in place, and Abbotts' own two-step on both Texas's bathroom *and* its sports bill.[413] [414] [415] [416]

This dynamic of hard-right but business-oriented governors trying to resist the worst impulses of their own newly MAGA-fied legislatures even ensnared Utah Gov. Cox, whose March 2022 sports bill veto was accom-panied by a headline-making statement of compassion: "75,000 high school kids participating in high school sports in Utah. Four transgender kids playing high school sports in Utah. One transgender student playing girls sports. 86% of trans youth reporting suicidality. 56% of trans youth having attempted suicide. Four kids and only one of them playing girls sports. That's what all of this is about. Four kids who aren't dominating or winning trophies or taking scholarships. Four kids who are just trying to find some friends and feel like they are a part of something. Four kids trying to get through each day. Rarely has so much fear and anger been directed at so few."

He would later add the following statement addressed to transgender children: "We care about you. We love you. It's going to be OK."[417] [418]

But they aren't loved, and it's not going to be okay.

The political ground is shifting rapidly, and Republican governors aren't sure exactly where to stand. They are trying to gauge where is too little and where will be just enough to satisfy the base's appetite for inflicting pain, especially on a sensitive subject like providing medical care to one's children. The problem is, that appetite is going to prove to be nearly bottomless.

2021 April

Gov. Hutchinson obligingly declares that he will gladly sign a clean anti-surgery bill, which is not saying much, because no gender affirming pediatric surgeries are actually being performed in his state.[419] No matter, the following day, April 7, Gov. Hutchinson's veto is crushed by the Republican super-majority in both houses, with a combined voted of 96 to 32. Arkansas is now the first state in the country to actually pass a law making gender-affirming medical care for trans youth illegal.

As legal scholar Ronald Krotoszynski would explain, "In Arkansas today… minors, with parents' consent, can obtain medically prescribed services or treatments for any other reason at all—just not this one."[420][421] He would add that "Since the 1970s, the Supreme Court has consistently rejected moral disapproval of a particular group of individuals as a constitutionally legitimate basis for imposing targeted legal burdens on the group…" This principle, which the Court relied on in landmark *Lawrence v. Texas,* it will be the central argument in all the federal anti-care lawsuits that will follow.

As Michele Hutchison recalled, "Severe, depression, suicidal ideation—all of it immediately sky-rocketed. Kids were terrified. Our staff would have to spend most of the day, just trying to talk them down. These legislators, many of whom had sat there while we testified, laughing in our faces, had set out to terrorize our children and unfortunately they succeeded."[422]

Arkansas's new measure is immediately challenged by the ACLU in the federal courts where District Judge James Moody issues an injunction stopping HB 1570 from ever going into effect. That dark honor still awaits Abbott and Texas. In August 2022 a three-judge panel of the 8th U.S. Circuit Court of Appeals refuses to revive HB 1570, and that November the full court votes overwhelming not to hear the state's appeal.[423] [424] [425]

As Strangio explains succinctly, "Parental rights apparently exist for everyone who doesn't want their kid to learn, or wear a mask, or get vaccinated. But they don't exist for parents who want to give their kids medically recommended care."[426]

2021 May

That same May, Huffines announces a primary challenge to Abbott (running for his third term) from the right. The problem is, there isn't a lot of room left there. But there are still three issues where Abbott is not quite as crazed as Huffines's extremist Freedom Caucus and thus still vulnerable to attack from the right, especially gay and transgender rights. Abbott reverses course on all of them, adopting every one of Huffines's positions. The days of freely-available gender affirming care in Texas clinics like GENECIS are now numbered.

There is a populist rebellion going on, the kind the US endures every few decades, and Texas politicians (like Republicans everywhere) are caught in its cross-hairs. Abbott started out as a standard-issue business Republican. But he is steadily being pushed rightward by both his Lt. Gov. Dan Patrick *and* his Atty. General, Ken Paxton, who keep subtly outflanking him. Despite his generally popularity with Republican voters, he will be primaried by no less than three opponents, all from his right including not only Huffines but his own Texas Republican State Party Chair.

Since Texas has not elected a Democrat to statewide office since 1994, there is no one pulling him left. There may be 16 million registered voters in Texas, but Republican candidates need just five percent of the 10% who show up for primaries to win office, and—as Texas Monthly explains—"[T]hey can't hope to win… without the support of the far-right base who reliably vote in primaries…."[427]

As with bathrooms and sports, the MAGA-fied right is now probing for the next vulnerability its War on Trans youth: there are trial balloons going up all over the state, as a key politician's test messages and tactics, gauging where the juice is with the evangelical right and what attacks on kids will have traction. And not only in Texas and Arkansas: that October, Kentucky will introduce an anti-care bill, and the following month Georgia law-makers will do the same. The rhythm of attack on gender-affirming care is gaining national momentum, as it moves slowly and inexorably into the center of the crosshairs.

Suddenly, everything seems to line up: Younger apparently has a lever he can pull to remake himself and the imaginary "chemical castration" of his daughter into a statewide issue (which might then be monetized); Huffines has Younger to use as stick to attack Abbott as soft on protecting Texas' kids; and the Freedom Caucus fin-ally realize they have a new issue that outrages the base.

White evangelical Christian nationalist groups like ADF and APP finally have the right time and place to start the anti-care phase of their religious crusade.[428] APP is about to announce that it is opening its first state chapter in Texas, with the explicit goal of building pressure on Abbott on trans issues.[429] [430] It will be followed by a $1m media campaign designed to force Abbott's hand on "protecting Texas kids" in a series of ads that feature…Jeff Younger.[431] One ad asks Texans; "When you were five what did you want to be when you grew up? A doctor? Maybe an astronaut? How about... the opposite sex? Right now corrupt doctors and big pharma are sexually transitioning our kids right here in Texas…."

Rightwing legislators' representatives officially ask A.G. Paxton to rule that hormone treatments are child abuse, and, as with Huffines's August 2021 request, he refuses to answer. Paxton still has his finger in the wind, and more than three months go by while he mulls his position.[432]

That same month, the Senate approves SB1311, which would revoke the license of any doctor for providing care to trans kids but Abbott's allies put it at the back of the legislative calendar and it never makes it up for a vote before the session ends. It is at least the third time the anti-care legislation has failed to advance in the Texas House, but it is one of the last times Abbott will moderate on trans issues.[433] [434]

2021 June

The ultra-right Freedom Caucus sends Abbott a letter insisting that he add anti-care to his legislative agenda. This is echoed by both Abbott's own state Republican Party of Texas and the evangelical Southern Baptists of Texas Convention, who explain, "Children must be saved from a lifetime of regret, sterility, and confusion. We must stop providers from being allowed to profit off our children." The reference to procreation, fertility, and sterility are not an accident.

Caucus leader Rep. Matt Krause then writes to GENECIS seeking details about the care it is providing to trans youth. Krause will shortly announce a challenge to Paxton for Attorney General. (Paxton has been indicted for securities fraud and is being investigated by the FBI after all *eight* members of his own senior staff accused him of corruption and were subsequently fired or resigned. This is the state's top law enforcement officer.)[435] [436] Abbott follows shortly with his own letter, and GENECIS' days are now clearly numbered.

2021 July

Rightwing radio host Mark Davis, perhaps channeling Huffines, presses Abbott on care, demanding: "Why, in a conservative state with Republicans in charge… a law that says we're not going to let you carve up your 10th grader because he thinks he's a girl—how in God's name does that not pass in Texas?"

Abbott responds by blaming the House and observing that chances of passage "are nil," without explaining that he is the likely cause of this. But ready to toss in the towel and go hard right on trans issues, he then ominously adds, "We have another solution that will address that problem that will be announced... within the next week."

Meanwhile, back in Dallas, Georgulas and Younger have attended another of their mandatory counseling sessions, but when one of the counselors addresses their daughter as "Luna," Younger allegedly stalks out for good. His refusal to continue attending these court-mandated sessions doom his custody rights. In an August hearing, District Court Judge Mary Brown (the recused Cooks' replacement) finds that Younger displays an "unwillingness or inability to follow the order designed to serve the best interests of the children."[437]

Never at fault for consistency, Younger has also allegedly failed to make his required child support payments, due in part to the fact that he is apparently once again largely unemployed. In a ruling rendered on August 3rd, Brown will grant Georgulas primary custody, exclusive rights to all psychiatric and health care — except blockers, hormones, or surgery, which require both parents' consent—as well as the all-important decision on Luna's hair length.

That same month, Huffines releases one of those dark, scary-voiced, apocalyptic ads so beloved on the right, accusing Abbott of "promoting transgender sexual policies to Texas youth."[438]

"Gov. Abbott's political appointees that are running the Department of Family and Protective Services have put out —and it's been on their website —some very disturbing information about our youth. They are

promoting transgender sexual policies to Texas youth. They're talking about helping empower and celebrate lesbian, gay, bisexual, transgender, queer, questioning, intersex, asexual, ally, non-heterosexual behavior. These are not Texas values. These are not Republican Party values, but these are obviously Greg Abbott's values."

Perhaps testing the limits of the electoral appeal of his new cause, Younger will shortly announce his own quixotic bid for the State House in which he will be crushed in the primary 38%-62%. Possibly echoing Younger's own charges, Huffines then accuses Abbott of not stopping the "mutilation" of Texas children, tweeting that August about the "Gender Identity and Sexual Orientation" section of the DFPS that contains suicide prevention information: *"It's offensive to see @GregAbbott TX use our tax dollars to advocate for transgender ideology. This must end."*

Trans issues have now reached such a fever pitch in Texas that within DFPS, this simple tweet is like setting off a bomb. It immediately ignites a department-wide panic and within 13 minutes, DFPS Media Relations Director Marissa Gonzales emails a link to the offending page to spokesman Patrick Crimmins with the subject: "Don Huffines video accusing Gov/DFPS of pushing liberal transgender agenda." She adds, "FYI this is blowing up on Twitter."

As with every other issue, the time frame of events in the war on transkids is compressed by the accelerant of social media. Crimmins contacts Web and Creative Director Darrell Azar who—like most of us who watched the 2016 election in bewilderment—is caught at the axis of a culture war he doesn't yet fully comprehend. Azar complains accurately if now pointlessly that the program has hosted LGBTQ+ content on its site "for as long as I can remember," including the offending page.

Nonetheless, within hours, the webpage disappears, along with the suicide prevention hotline. Just to leave no flank exposed to Huffines's attack, DFPS also takes down the entire website for Texas Youth Connection, a division that steers foster care youth to resources on things like education, housing… and of course its own now-non-existent LGBTQ+ page.[439]

2021 August

Apparent seeking ammunition to use against him in the A.G. race, Krause now sends a letter asking Paxton whether affirming-care constitutes child abuse. It's yet another trial balloon to test tactics and messages. Nonetheless, Paxton will take more than half a year to reply. The ground is shifting under him too, but unlike Abbott, Paxton is apparently still trying to decide the right place to stand.

Abbott sends his own letter, asking for an official legal determination as to whether GAC-related surgeries are child abuse. The letter only mentions "surgical procedure that will sterilize the child, such as orchiectomy or hysterectomy, or remove otherwise healthy body parts, such as penectomy or mastectomy." Again, the reference to procreation is not accidental. His letter makes no mention of puberty blockers or hormone treatment or gender-affirming social transition. Abbott is still trying to find the line he needs to cross that will satisfy the mob. He won't find it, because there isn't one.

Abbott's letter also contains specific exception for procedures that are part of Intersex Genital Mutilation, and which the state is at pains to continue.[440] In fact, without a hint of irony, AG Paxton would later unfavorably compare gender-affirming care *to* intersex mutilation.

What is happening here is that access to medical care for a transgender 14-year-old girl in Lubbock or a 15-year-old boy in El Paso and tens of thousands like them is now being decided in a bunch of petty, tit-for-tat political maneuvers among a handful of politicians, trying to one-up one another in posturing before the white evangelical Christian base. In effect, the five to 10% of Republicans who vote in the primary, are now deciding young people's access to affirming care for the entire state.

2021 October

Abbott's now turns his attention to GENECIS.

Just two months earlier, Children's Medical Center Dallas had pointed out for a journalist that GENECIS saw 500 transgender young people in 2021 and that it was vital for their health, reducing their "significant suffering and extraordinarily high suicide." According to Ximena Lopez, although they are now being publicly attacked by Younger and the rightwing group, Protect Texas Kids, the hospital believes it best to take a passive stance, stay with the medical facts, and maintain political neutrality, because the uproar will blow over

Based on their past seven years of experience, this is not an unreasonable strategy: but these are no longer reasonable times. The political climate has just changed completely changed in the past few months. University of

Texas Southwestern Hospital and Children's Medical Center Dallas who jointly manage the clinic, are now in the hotseat and things are only going to go downhill, so their *wait-and-see* strategy turns out to be the worst possible choice.

First up is a bill in the Texas legislature. In his public testimony, Younger takes direct aim at GENECIS, despite the fact that his daughter was not a patient and did not receive any treatment, declaring that: "After a $1,000,000 court battle, I very narrowly averted having my son sent to the GENECIS Clinic in Dallas, Texas to be chemically castrated. GENECIS currently has a pipeline of over 300 children that are prepubescent. I don't know how many are pubescent—we didn't get that in discovery—but we know that they have 300 prepubescent kids in the pipeline…"

Almost none of this is true. But no one involved with the hospital defends GENECIS. As Lopez, who has been banned from speaking officially as well, explains afterwards, "I had this responsibility for my kids, my patients, but I couldn't speak about them: it was like I was witnessing a crime but I couldn't speak out about it."[441][442]

Then Abbott announces at an event later that month, "…I think everybody here can agree that gender modification by surgical procedure is physical abuse of a child…I just talked to the person who is the head of the Texas Department of Family and Protective Services, so that's the Child Protection Agency. And I asked her to define child abuse as including surgical sexual change procedure of a minor."

A spokesperson for Children's Medical and U.T. Southwestern refuse to confirm or deny that they've been contacted by Abbott, but a likely translation is: *The Governor told us if we don't pull the plug on GENECIS, our state funding and maybe even our medical license may mysteriously disappear.*

GENECIS, the groundbreaking program opened in 2014 by Lopez to such fanfare, closes its doors in November 2021. Children's Hospital and U.T. take down its website, and scrub their own of any mention of "gender affirming" or "transgender," so that families or young people searching for information will find nothing.

From this point until a temporary injunction enables GENECIS to reopen the following year in May, 2022, over 100 children and families seeking treatment are turned away.

U.T. issues a bizarre public statement that the clinic has not been "closed, but rather removing the GENECIS program brand was made to provide a more private experience for patients and families." Which is a bit like saying, "We closed our program so it could provide better treatment."

But the purge doesn't stop there.

A few months later in early 2022, U.T. leadership removes all mentions of the words "transgender" or "gender dysphoria" from its teaching syllabus, as well as the printed course description for an elective class *on* transgender issues.[443] In full reverse mode and touching every base to satisfy the governor, they then change the course title from "Adolescent and Young Adult Transgender Care" to "Multidisciplinary Care of Diverse Youth"... before finally killing it altogether and removing the course as an available medical school elective.

Just four months after GENECIS is closed, Texas

Children's Hospital and Legacy Community Center (both in Houston) both stop providing medical care.[444] [445]

2021 November

Rightwing legislators' representatives officially ask A.G. Paxton to rule that hormone treatments are child abuse, and as with Huffines's August 2021 request, he refuses to answer. Paxton still has his finger in the wind, and more than three months go by while he still mulls his position.[446]

2021 December

Paxton finally makes his mind up and decides like Abbott that he will go all in. His opening salvo is pretty small, attacking Endo Pharmaceuticals and AbbVie Inc, for advertising puberty blockers as gender dysphoria treatments although the FDA has not approved them for this.[447] [448] The days of available affirming care for Texas' teens has only a matter of days left.

2022 February

The end dawns on the morning of February 18th when Paxton issues his notorious Opinion No. KP-0401, a "non-binding legal opinion" that reinterprets §261.001 of the Texas Family Code to redefine gender-affirming care as criminal child abuse.

In *Sex Is as Sex Does*, scholar Paisley Currah's exploration of the different definitions of sex used by states and even among different agencies within the same state, he explains: "[S]ex is whatever an entity whose decisions are backed by the force of law says it is... [S]ex is a mobile property-dependent not on what it is, but what it does..."[449]

Paxton's Opinion adopts this same legal posture regarding child abuse in Texas: *It is what we say it is.* And as with sex, the point isn't what child abuse *is*, but rather what child abuse can be made to *do.*[450]

Paxton's Opinion No. KP-0401 is released as a belated response to Rep. Matt Krause's outstanding inquiry back on August 2021. It is now more than six months afterwards, and Paxton and Abbott have apparently both at last found the political ground they will stand on.[451]

The Opinion opens with a gratuitous nod to the "*sterilization of minors and other vulnerable populations without clear consent is not a new phenomenon and has an unsettling history. Historically weaponized against minorities, sterilization procedures have harmed many vulnerable populations, such as African Americans, female minors, the disabled.* Any mention of the injustices historically visited on the state's women and minorities is particularly hurtful, since one the main perpetrators of this has been...the state itself."[452]

But the legal opinion is markedly odd for other reasons. The actual medical procedures which are supposedly the issue are only mentioned once, it its opening two pages. It devotes almost all of its remaining 13 single-spaced pages to ensuring that transgender youth are never robbed of their ability to procreate, which is mentioned 45 times—including 10 times on one single page:

"...providing these elective sex changes... perm-
anently sterilizes those minor children...beyond
the obvious harm of permanently sterilizing a
child...the fundamental right at stake: the right
to procreate... impair their ability to procreate...
irreversible sterilization...high rate of regret at
being sterilized...infringe on upon a minor
child's constitutional right to procreate...."

The Opinion explains that, *"No doctor can replace*
a fully functioning male sex organ with a fully functioning
female sex organ (or vice versa) [and] these "sex
change" procedures seek to destroy a fully functioning
sex organ..." In one bizarre footnote, it even identifies the
main issue around top-surgery not as "mutilation, " but
rather one of *"altering a minor female's breasts in such a*
way that it would prevent that minor female from having
the ability to breast-feed her eventual children."

In other words, KP-0401 is a love letter to the
evangelical Christian nationalist right generally, and APP
specifically.[453] As such, it is a kind of Rosetta Stone for
translating the evangelical Christian nationalist obsession
with eradicating gender "deviants" in the cause of
preserving heterosexual fertility and childbirth.[454]

In a similar vein, KP-0401 echoes Texas' unfortunate history of embracing "positive eugenics:" an early
20th century movement that used the state to manipulate
families' reproductive practices.[455] [456] [457] In Texas this
included preventing white intermarriage with its Black
and brown citizens, controlling the fertility of the
"mentally unfit," and promoting reproduction among its
white, heterosexual, propertied Christian families.

In fact, like other states in the early 1900s, Texas even promoted "Fitter Family Contests," at popular county fairs, in which doctors would conduct psychological and physical examinations of each member of competing families and awarded the winners a trophy—only a paddock or two away from those being awarded for the healthiest steer or the biggest heifer.[458]

Curiously, nowhere in the Opinion does Paxton actually challenge the basic facts of being transgender: i.e., that people are born with gender identities, that for some these are contrary to the sex assigned at birth, and that this causes some to experience gender dysphoria.

In this connection, it is worth noting that that Amber Briggle—who will become of the parents harassed by CPS because of Paxton's opinion and is about to become a named plaintiff in the ACLU's lawsuit against him and Abbott—publicly invited Paxton over for dinner in 2016 after testifying against the bathroom bill. Briggle wanted Paxton to meet her (then) eight year-old child M.B.

To her surprise, Paxton actually accepted. And then to Briggle's further astonishment, he actually showed up with his wife and bearing a homemade dessert in hand. Before dinner, he went off to wash his hands with M.B., reportedly saying, "This is nice. It's been a while since I had kids this age." Then they all sat down and enjoyed a congenial dinner together.

Briggle's theory apparently was that *It's hard to hate up close.* Even four years later when M.B. is fully-grown, she still thinks, "If they just *meet* him, they'll see how amazing he is. It's hard to deny when he's standing there in front of you."[459]

It's a good theory, but in this case it's wrong.[460]

142

She was one of many such parents I spoke with who felt that if only legislators could get to know them and their children, they would realize that all the ADF and APP hate-literature was completely wrong, and they would stop. As one very active Texas mom, who has testified with her daughter in Austin many times would explain out, "When we went up there and testified in 2017 they knew nothing about transgender. But by the end of that session, they knew exactly what they were doing. They just didn't' care."[461] [462] Possibly some legislators are likely not haters at all, while others probably are. But all of them need to satisfy the mob, and like all the mobs, it won't be satisfied unless there is blood.

As one bewildered and frightened Texas mom who had been doxed, received death threats, followed to work by men in cars (including by one who pulled a gun), and called "groomer" and "pedophile" more times than she could count explained to me: *We're not interesting. That's why I tell people: 'I don't know why you're so interested in me. I'm your typical boring American mom. I work. I watch some TV. I foster puppy dogs and cats. And when my kid comes out of his room, we sometimes have some good conversations about nothing in particular.'"* But after several years of this, she and her trans son so feared for their lives that they were moving to New Zealand.[463]

Abbott immediately follows Paxton's Opinion with his own letter, instructing DFPS to begin investigating families who get medical care for their trans children. It is now official.

DFPS is an especially unfortunate choice for an enforcement mechanism, since it is tragically understaffed and continuously in crisis by design. because Republicans don't care about the predominantly Black and brown children in its care. In 2015, a federal judge would note that "Rape, abuse, psychotropic medication, and instability are the norm" at DFPS, and the following year a study would fine that two hundred children had died tragically of maltreatment in its care.[464] It is designed to designed to pass kids along to a chain of mostly white evangelical-dominated agencies and volunteer families whom the state counts on to provide the bulk of its foster care. Gay and transgender kids are highly over-represented, but many are still sent to families and agencies that try to *Pray the Gay Away.*

Child Protective Services (CPS), its investigative arm, is similarly underfunded and in disorganized. Nearly a year after the judge's 2015 ruling, it still had not visited nearly 5,000 children classified as *high risk* of immanent harm.

In the midst of this deadly chaos, CPS's top priority is now investigating happy families caring for their transgender children. And they *are* prioritized.

As Abbott's order is issued, a mother with a 16-year-old transgender daughter who works at DFPS goes to see her supervisor, asking what the effect the order will have on her and her. Within hours, she is placed on administrative leave. And then *the very next day*, a CPS investigator calls on her.[465] [466] Strangely enough, the episode unintentionally provides an object lesson in what the state's politicians *could* do to stop the worst cases of child abuse and early death, if they actually cared to do so.

In many cases, CPS investigators just show up on families' doorstep, demanding to investigate them. In other cases, CPS shows up at their child's school unannounced to take the child off to a closed room for inter-rogation without their family's knowledge or consent. One parent would train her non-binary son to say: "I don't want to talk to you without my lawyer present."[467]

As detailed in the *Washington Post,* one CPS investigator who is given a trans family to investigate for abuse is 52-year-old, Morgan Davis—who has just transitioned himself just 10 months earlier.[468]

Davis already has an unmanageable docket of 25 cases of actual abuse, but he hopes that he can do the investigation as gently as possible—convinced that he is the most sympathetic investigator the family could get—and then quietly close the case. While at the house, the daughter asks him with a child's artlessness, "Do you want to see my room?" She doesn't understand that he's there to investigate her for being trans like himself, and possibly to take her away from her room, her home, and her family. And this realization nearly reduces him to tears on the spot. Davis will spend much of the following weekend crying, determined to file a positive report that closes the matter out.

Only later, after reporting that the family was "exemplary" and "impeccable" in every way, will Davis learn that transgender cases *cannot be closed,* that he cannot issue a finding of *no abuse.*[469]

Davis is now caught in the familiar double-bind of decent people dealing with the indecent and inhumane policies enacted by the MAGA right: Stay and try to mitigate the harm and become complicit, or leave with the certain knowledge that your replacement will be much worse. To this day, I know of no moral calculus by which one might solve this equation.

As he is leaving the home of another loving family doing their best to raise their transgender child, their lawyer will draw him aside and say: "You shouldn't be here. I know you mean well, but this is wrong. You shouldn't do this." She is right, and Davis quits.

He joins a flood of resignations by CPS staff who had joined because they genuinely care about children, and cannot bear to be a part of what they considered a political stunt that only hurts, humiliates, and frightens the very children they're supposed to be helping.[470] [471]

Many parents begin assembling "safe books" kept close at hand which contain official letters from every therapist who has evaluated their child, forms documenting the diagnoses of doctors providing any care, letters from their pediatrician, and certified copies of official documents like birth certificates and name-changes.[472] They patiently answer CPS's questions, let investigators poke around their homes, and allow them to interview their children alone, convinced—like Briggle's inviting Paxton for dinner—that once they see the truth, it will become clear that it's all just a horrible mistake.

But it's not a mistake, and no one is interested in the truth.

And as this becomes apparent, families begin withdrawing their cooperation and lawyer-up. From here on, all CPS inquiries will be directed to family attorneys who will stonewalled all requests for information and be on-hand when CPS shows up for home inspections. The brief honeymoon of cooperation is over, and these families are now fully aware that they are in a battle for their lives. Not only are their children in danger of being taken away from them and forcibly de-transitioned socially and medically, but the parents are in violation of the law and thus in danger of being imprisoned for felony child abuse.

And as this sinks in Texas, families begin fleeing across its borders.[473]

Which seems to be just what Abbott wants—so that none of them will provide more political ammunition to Huffines and the evangelical Christian right. One single mother who was leaving the state was asked by CPS investigator to let them know once she had crossed the state line, because once she was out Texas, they had no more interest in her alleged *child abuse*.

I interviewed one mom who remains a prominent pro-trans activist in one of the state's largest cities. She explained that in her experience, it was mostly parents who called out Abbott or Paxton by name on social media or in the press who were targeted by CPS. So she never criticizes any official by name, is very careful what she posts online, and makes sure to keep her public comments constructive. (In addition, she is fortunate enough to live in a county where the head of CPS has declared he won't investigate, and the local DA has declared he won't prosecute.)

The evangelical half-sister of another single mom was venomously opposed to her affirming her transgender daughter. She would anonymously notify CPS of one complaint after another: one claiming the mother was mentally ill and endangering her child, another that she was buying hormones online illegally, and so on. Even as the mother was struggling to close out one complaint, CPS would open an investigation into another. Finally she realized that she couldn't win whatever game she was stuck in, so she packed up, and left for good. The way Abbott has structured his ban. anyone can drop a dime on an affirming parent—a disgruntled neighbor, an anti-gay family member, a fellow church-goer, even a hostile school teacher.

One single mother I spoke with fled overnight after being advised by her lawyer that a CPS staffer assigned to her case had taken an unexpectedly aggressive posture. She packed up their three children, two lizards, and three cats and drove for four days and nights—stopping off along the interstate only to sleep in their van—until they reached Connecticut, a sanctuary state. There they lived out of the van for three more weeks in the middle of the winter, while the kids went to school during the day and she delivered Walmart packages to feed them all. Once in a while, some kind stranger would get them a motel room or they would have enough in their GoFundMe to buy it themselves so they could all shower and sleep in warm beds for a change. Eventually the local queer community found them a place to live, but shortly after she was hospitalized with severe chest pains from the stress.[474]

Most parents told harrowing stories of leaving behind extended families and lifelong friends, of careers overturned, forced sales of their homes at a fraction of their true value, of life savings and retirement accounts drained or simply left behind. It is the kind of boundless love all of us hope for from a parent, but too few of us actually experience. Many were life-long Texans who could never safely return—even to visit family or friends—until their transgender child was fully grown.

And maybe not even then. One parent told of a CPS investigator who continued pursuing her even after her child was an adult and no longer living at home. He took the position that the alleged abuse had happened while the child was a minor and thus still in her care. Finally, she realized his point was not the "abuse," but finding a pretext to take away her state social worker's license. So she left, too.

Weirdly enough, these transgender children were the "lucky" ones. The situation would be infinitely worse for those from low-income families that couldn't afford to leave or pay for out-of-state care, as well as for the many trans and genderqueer youth in the state's juvenile probation and foster care system—who were disproportionately Black, brown and LGBTQ+—and whose parents couldn't, or wouldn't, fight for their right to care.

The parents I interviewed were almost invariably straight, working class, church-going, and gender-normative. Many were life-long Republicans and most had had no contact with the LGBTQ+ community until their kid came out and they found themselves immersed in a crash course on Transgender 101, trying to understand why the child they loved was so distraught and following medical advice on how to help them.

Amber Briggle was the only Texas parent investigated by CPS who has remained defiantly in-state, vocal, and active. She spoke about how she and her husband created an Emergency Exit Plan that included keeping pet carriers stocked and ready, their car fully gassed up, and a mapped route to the nearest state line in case they got that call in the night from their lawyers saying that their time was up.[475] [476] Briggle would ask rhetorically, "Now that [Texas] is criminalizing parents, who is going to speak?"

But that seems to be the point. The message being sent by Abbott and Paxton appears to be: *Keep your head*

*down and your mouth shut and you might get by; become
an issue and we will come for your child.*

Neither DFPS nor CPS has ever released a full
accounting of cases opened, but the number most often
cited as of this writing is 19, which sounds suspiciously
low. To my knowledge, there have been no reports of CPS
actually forcing any family under investigation to stop
providing hormones, or actually charging any with felony
child abuse, transgender children actually taken into
custody for receiving affirming care, or even being directly
threatened by CPS with having their child removed.

Of course, there's no guarantee that this will not
occur in the future. But what this looks like most is a
campaign of terror to silence those families already
providing care, intimidate new ones into not seeking it,
and stop doctors and therapists from providing it.[477]

This strategy will be reflected in the coming
avalanche of overly-broad, badly-worded bills which are
about to be introduced in the state legislature. As
transgender minister Remington Johnson told me, "These
bills are badly drawn with a purpose: because the more that
can be read into them, the more they terrorize parents, who
aren't sure what they mean or how they might be used
against them. And that drives down the number of families
willing to risk providing care to their trans* kids."[478]

It is possible that for Abbott's political agenda,
stopping short of actual child removal accomplishes what
he needs, providing less legal liability or political exposure
from the state's many unhappy Fortune 500s, while
placating his extremist evangelical base. This is also what
CPS—*not* the local police or county sheriffs who could
have been tapped to do the investigations— appears to be
doing: wielding its tools of surveillance, interrogation,

demands for personal records, and the adrenalin panic of intrusive and unannounced home inspection.[479]

As Texas ACLU attorney Brian Klosterboer noted, the fear and confusion are not a by-product but the point. "We see teachers, nurses, and therapists—all worried that they should report children or actually doing so. And all of this acts to intimidate and suppresses providing critical care and support for transgender youth. If you're a parent considering starting care for the first time, this order and the fear surrounding it risks shutting the door. It is harming young people across the state."[480]

2022 March

ACLU and Lambda Legal immediately file suit against Abbott, and the action now shifts to federal court in Travis County. The case will first be heard by a trail judge, and then go up down the ladder of appellate courts, before these are exhausted and it ends up at the State Supreme Court or—in cases that raising constitutional issues—the U.S. Supreme Court. Lawyers from these two nonprofits will shortly be crisscrossing the country, filing and arguing in state after state, forming the bulwark of transkids' defense. It is impossible to overstate their contributions.

ACLU and Lambda's first motion is for a temporary injunction on behalf of the DFPS mother with the 16-year-old daughter who was placed on administrative leave and then investigated the day after Abbott's E.O. As is usual, they are assisted by a local law firm licensed to practice in the state, in this case the prestigious, 700-lawyer firm of Baker Botts. Over time, big law firms employ a variety of people, and among those who had worked at Baker Botts's include ultra-right Trump Supreme Court appointee, Amy

Coney Barrett, virulently transphobic Sen. Ted Cruz (who is tweeting about "child abuse"), and former-President George W. Bush, who perhaps appropriately never worked at any higher position than the company mailroom.[481]

As the lead plaintiff, Jane Does appears in court disguised wearing glasses and wig. and the court blocks the live video feed of her testimony. She testifies that her family now lives in "constant fear," and her teenage daughter is unable to sleep at night because she is "traumatized by the prospect that she could be separated from her parents and lose access to medical treatment…"[482]

At the hearing, Paxton's Assistant A.G., Ryan Kercher, blandly argues that "These treatments could be used by somebody to harm a child," adding helpfully that "affirming is not always abuse, and that the state won't investigate parents simply because their child is receiving treatment." Kercher adds condescendingly: "Despite the frankly breathless media coverage of these important issues, there has been no call to investigate all trans youth or all youth undergoing these gender affirming procedures or therapies. That's not the case…"[483]

He is wrong. Within 48-hours, Paxton publicly contradicts his own A.A.G., tweeting that, "When performed on children… puberty blockers, and hormone therapies are 'abuse' under Texas law. They're illegal." Kercher is gone by the time the case is heard on appeal.[484] [485]

The ACLU's brief argues that Abbott and Paxton have no legislative authority to refine the law, that their actions circumvent a legislature (which had numerous opportunities to pass just such a law), that they have singled out transgender families for harassment, and that they are endangering the health and well-being of young people who are simply following the best medical advice.

In addition, while Arkansas' law (stayed by the courts) may have also sought to criminalize care, Texas is the only state in the country threatening to take children from families and place them into foster care.

The roster of plaintiffs in the case includes father and husband *John Doe*, their 16-year-old daughter *Mary Doe*, and Houston psychologist, Dr. Megan Mooney, who argues that the new policy forces her to report her clients or else face the loss of her license and civil or possibly even criminal penalties. Echoing the quote from scholar Jules Gill-Peterson that opens this chapter, she declares simply, "When a child tells you who they are, believe them."[486] The same day, HRC and 60 corporate allies drop the first ad in a state-wide "Discrimination is Bad for Business" campaign."[487][488]

2022 June

On the 6th, a host of additional plaintiffs join the ACLU's *Doe v. Abbott* lawsuit, including activist Amber Briggle and her 14-year-old transgender son M.B.; *Samantha Poe* and her 13-year-old nonbinary child *Whitley Poe*; *Wanda Roe* and her 16-year-old son *Tommy Roe*; and *Mirabel Voe* and their 16-year-old son *Antonio Voe*.[489][490][491]

Antonio reads about the situation online and tries to kill himself. He is taken to a nearby emergency room, where his is briefly hospitalized. Once discharged, the staff report his family to CPS for possible child abuse. It is unclear if this is out of malice or because it is now a matter of state law. What is clear is that when CPS shows up on *Voe's* doorstep, they will fail to express any interest or concern over *Antonio's* recent suicide attempt (which their impending investigation helped precipitate) and focus solely on his gender-affirming care.

This is another consequence of the Abbott-Paxton policy: any transchild sees a doctor, dentist, or therapist, or even goes to school in their correct gender now faces the threat of being reported and investigated. In fact, it is now the *legal responsibility* of such professionals, who are themselves exposed to civil or criminal liability if they fail to do so.

In effect, being publicly out as a transgender minor is now just short of a crime.

In Travis County, Judge Amy Clark Meachum grants a temporary injunction against DFPS pending a full trial in July, just four months later.

Within the hour, Abbott appeals. As the appellant, his argument makes for interesting reading. It stands on four main arguments as to why the injunction should be lifted and shouldn't have been granted to begin with.[492] First, it denies that the plaintiffs even have any cause of action against DFPS, which deserves no explanation or comment.

Second, it argues that in order for DFPS to be outside its statutory authority, plaintiffs have to show that providing puberty blockers and hormone treatment *never* creates a risk to a child's health. This is a strange argument to make, since providing *aspirin* to children carries well-documented health risks.

Third, the appeal argues that Meachum's injunction is unnecessary because DFPS is merely investigating and has no authority to interfere with parents' private medical decisions nor has it ever claimed to. To the untrained eye, it might seem that threatening to take a child from their parents to prevent them from taking hormones or blockers does indeed interfere with parental decision-making.

Finally, it argues that there is no evidence that plaintiffs face "imminent, irreparable harm." Again, speaking solely here as a non-lawyer, having one's child taken away and put with an anonymous church-based family in the foster care system and then being civilly or criminally charged with child abuse seem pretty imminent and harmful to me.

As regards PFLAG specifically, the appeal argues that its stated mission of creating "a caring, just, and affirming world for LGBTQ+ people and those who love them" is unrelated to the "concerns of a few of its members about being found to have abused their children." It's impossible to explain the logic of this argument, so I won't try.

The sum of Abbott's appeal is: *Nothing to see here: just business as usual.*

Perhaps the most generous way to think about this document is that the incoming A.A.G. who has replaced the late, unlamented Ryan Kercher has been asked to put the same lipstick on the same pig—which is what lawyers do for clients with losing cases. It often doesn't work, and it doesn't work here either.

Finding that plaintiffs in both cases have "a probable right to relief sought," the Court of Appeals for the Third Judicial District in Austin upholds not only Meachum's original injunction, but extends its ambit further to include the entire state. It then remands both cases back to Judge Meachum to be heard that July, as originally scheduled.

This ruling halts all active CPS investigations. Abbott immediately appeals yet again, this time to the Texas State Supreme Court.

2022 May

Meanwhile, on May 12, Dallas County Judge Melissa Bellan issues a temporary injunction allowing Ximena Lopez and GENECIS to reopen their doors. Within hours five new patients register. Judge Bellan finds that Child-ren's Medical Center has broken the law by "interfering with doctors' pro-fessional judgment, discriminating against patients because of their gender identity" and by forcing Lopez to do so as well.[493]

The following day, the Texas Supreme Court upholding Meachum's finding that Abbott's actions harmed plaintiffs and keeps the temporary injunction in place for *Doe, Poe, Roe, Voe,* Megan Mooney, and PFLAG. To say that this Court is unfriendly to transgender interests would be an understatement, so this is not insignificant. However, it also finds the appellate court lacked the authority to make its temporary injunction statewide, and that it can only protect actions against these named plaintiffs. So all Texas parents not named once again at risk, and will have to file their own suits to get relief. As one family's lawyer will remark, "I tell people: God and CPS, those are the two entities that have the power to give you children and take them away. So these investigations are a big deal."[494]

Employing the same tortured logic it applied seven years earlier to keep alive the repeal of Houston's HERO Act, the Court finds that while "the Governor and the Attorney General were certainly well within their rights to state their legal and policy views on this topic, DFPS was not compelled by law to follow them."[495] In other words: *these are just the personal opinions of the state's Governor and its chief law enforcement officer and there's no legal requirement that DFPS must follow them.* They hardly need add —*even though they are your bosses, can fire you tomorrow, and control the budget, the policies, and the management of your department.*

This confuses nearly everyone, as families and lawyers for the nine known open investigations wait to see how DFPS will react. The Court has given it an exit ramp if it wants one, but since the entire upper manage-ment are Abbott political appointees, why would it? Sure enough, less than a week later, DFPS contacts the lawyers for all the families who are not named plaintiffs in *Doe v Abbott* or *PFLAG v Abbott* to inform them that their investigations are resuming.[496]

The TRO for *Abbott v PFLAG* prevents investigation of families who are PFLGA members, but exactly how it will work in practice is neither specified nor entirely clear. Does a parent have to be a PFLAG member *before* the investigation starts, or can they join *after* they are being investigated? What if they *were* members, but then had let it their membership lapse?

According to the Texas ACLU's Klosterboer, how the TRO has worked in practice is that when a family is notified they are being investigated or fears an investigation is imminent, they must hire an attorney, who then gives DFPS proof that they're PFLAG members. As of this writing, DFPS has not yet challenged any family's PFLAG membership, and it has paused or closed all investigations involving PFLAG members.

The net effect is, for the time being all investigations under Abbott's order have been blocked for PFLAG members and their families throughout the state. But for any parent with a transgender child, the fear and doubt that it could all come apart tomorrow with a single stroke of the Courts' pen is still there, causing fear and chaos and suppressing care.[497] And parents in more remote parts of the state who are unaware of the ruling, or fail to hire lawyers are or unable to, still remain completely at risk of investigation and/or felony charges for loving their kids.

Texas now stands alone as the first and only state both banning and criminalizing the providing of medical care to transgender children. As the Kaiser Family Foundation noted, other states would propose policies that limited care or proposed penalties for parents. But none put forth laws that made parental love into felony child abuse like Texas, or made community members responsible for reporting suspect parents to authorities.[498]

Reportedly, white Christian nationalist organizations like ADF and APP had specifically selected Texas as their starting point because—as the second most populous state and $2.3 trillion in GDP—it was likely to be unboycottable. The evangelical Christian right had been circling the gay community, probing for new weaknesses, and identifying fresh avenues of attack. Internalizing the lessons of *Obergefell* and North Carolina, they had adapted. And their efforts were rewarded with astonishing success. Just like the Connecticut lawsuit against Miller, it doesn't matter that Texas' efforts are half-assed and incomplete. A climate of fear and backlash had been created that dramatically reduced teen transitions and the availability of trans medical care while profoundly suppressed the social visibility of transgender youth.[499]

Neither the left nor the nation as a whole realizes it, but the kind of anti-care ban the right piloted in Texas was qualitatively and quantitatively different from anything that had gone before. Sports bans affected less than a hundred kids: medical bans affected tens of thousands. No one fled a state overnight because their child couldn't play kickball. But whole families left states like Texas, Georgia, Idaho, North Dakota, and Tennessee because of the threat of criminal prosecution and having their children taken away from them. Being unable to play a school sport may have been painful, but it was nothing compared to watching helplessly as your body was forced to undergo the wrong puberty because of involuntary hormone poisoning that was easily preventable.

Sports bills and bathroom bills banned something trans kids *did:* anti-care bills banned something they *were.* They attempted to legislatively erase transgender children from existence, as evidenced in the flood of successive bans on everything from using the correct name or pronouns, to changing names or birth certificates or even wearing the right clothes. This fight now isn't about whether a few trans girls can try out for track or use the women's room: it's whether about 60,000+ trans kids are going to lose access to life-saving medical care and their right to legally *be* transgender. (See Appendix D). As APP president Schilling explained, "I view [care] the same as I view lobotomies or eugenics—it's a bad medical fad," and therefore the APP's goal is "ending *all* affirming care so that transition care is thought of as a horrific medical practice that happened in the past.[500]"

In other words, eradicating transgender completely.

Ninety percent of the hundreds of anti-trans bills introduced from 2019 through 2022 would fail to pass. Even those that passed the more MAGA-oriented Houses would often die quietly in the more business-oriented Senate chambers. A few of the remaining 10% of bills that did pass, would be vetoed.

But the rest make it into law. Many are then tied up

in lawsuits and eventually stayed by federal judges or by appellate courts.[501]

But the net effect is, across half of the country, often the sole institution standing between transgender children and their administrative, medical, and legal eradication is the federal courts. This is not an insignificant obstacle.

Evangelical Christian nationalist groups like ADF, APP, Heritage, and FRC are expert at whipping up fear and exploiting the resulting moral panic. But the courts—even red state ones stocked with far-right judges—generally require some sort of factual evidence to back up claims. And hysteria about something and hatred towards it are not admissible evidence.

Yet this is a slender thread on which to hang the hopes of half a country's worth of traumatized and dysphoric kids.

But it is all they have.

Because except for a handful of outmatched Democratic legislators, the ACLU and Lambda, and LGBT+ rights groups, the rest of society will turn its gaze away, leaving them hanging there, fighting for their lives, twisting slowly in the political winds.

Epilogue

In 2016, the entire country had rallied around transgender people. Trans rights had been ascendant, even victorious. As HRC had triumphantly announced, McCrory's sudden and absolute defeat in a highly conservative state, had proven that there was no longer an appetite for legislative expressions of hatred towards LGBTQ+[502], Red state Republicans had absorbed the lesson, and were now gun-shy of ever attacking us again.

But barely half a dozen years later the world had turned upside down. And Texas wasn't imposing some minor fine like North Carolina for using the "wrong" restroom: it was mounting a brazen and unconstitutional frontal assault on transgender kids by wielding the heavy-hand of state-sponsored witch hunts and criminalization of affirming parents. Within two years, half the states would follow Texas's lead.[503] [504]

What the hell happened?

The simple answer is, as APP had planned all along, was that Republican politicians got comfortable with attacking gay people again, as long as the used trans people to tap the evangelical Christian nationalist base's unending fear and loathing for queers.[505] APP reportedly investing over $5m into their efforts. They learned that as long as they confined their attacks to transgender kids—

about which the society was still ambivalent and unwilling to strike back—they could do so with impunity

The more complex answer is, the rest of the country generally, and the progressive left in particular, failed to react. All the various forces that came together so brilliantly in North Carolina to support transgender adults' rights to use a bathroom disappeared when it came to the right of transgender kids to *be* transgender kids. There would be no backlash, no calls for boycotts.

It was the dog that didn't bark.

Researcher Chloe Souchere and I looked at public statements from a cross-section of 18 largest and most high-profile civil society, civil rights, and women's rights groups. Nearly 100% made public statements in support of abortion rights and gay marriage. However, that figure plummeted to less than half (44%) for youth affirming care.[506] [507]

And the volume of their statements dropped as well, from about 70 statements in support of abortion rights and of gay marriage to a meagre 10 for care—a decline of 84%.[508] [509] [510]

For another comparison, when gay marriage panics swept red-state America, 15 states enacted their own protections through gay marriage, civil union, or domestic partnership laws. In the aftermath of *Roe v Wade* being overturned, 10 states have passed abortion sanctuary laws and/or expanded their existing abortion protections.[511]

But so far, just three states have passed sanctuary laws that guarantee trans kids and their families the right to affirming medical care.[512]

In effect, if a 15-year-old girl gets pregnant and wants an abortion, the entire civil rights/civil society community has her back. But if that same 15-year-old announces that he is transgender and that he wants to go on hormone blockers to halt his menstrual period and stop his breasts from developing, the civil rights community will largely sit on its hands.

And so will the rest of society. As families were overnight began fleeing Texas in terror, the NCCA and the NBA didn't pull any championships. The Boss and Maroon 5 didn't cancel any shows. Major corporations didn't announced the cancellation of multi-million dollar expansions and major entertainment companies didn't halt any planned productions.[513] Michael Jordan, the Beatles, and the Boss didn't go to the mat over *trannies.*

And Attorney General Merrick Garland didn't take to the nation's airwaves at Biden's request to assure transgender children that "We see you."

On the contrary, unlike Obama's bold action on trans bathrooms and school sports, Biden—supposedly the most pro-LGBTQ+ president ever—signed a completely toothless E.O., then announced piously "You are loved. You are heard."[514] [515]

But they weren't, and he didn't. Just weeks later, Biden's administration gave its blessing to states' banning trans adolescents from competitive high school and college sports.[516] [517] We had gone from Loretta Lynch's stirring and impassioned public embrace of transgender as a civil rights issue to the emptiness of performative politics at its worst.[518] [519]

In fact, as the War on Trans youth unfolded, no major segment of society beyond the LGBTQ+ community, the ACLU, and a handful of over-matched Democrats in statehouses, has taken emphatic action.[520]

This has allowed the mainstream media to push a narrative that there is a valid "both sides" controversy here, as major outlets like the *New York Times, Atlantic, Ms. Magazine, The Economist,* BBC, and *The Nation* publish piece after piece on the "problem" of care and the lack of professional consensus.

But there is none. All 27 professional organizations providing pediatric care have endorsed it as safe and effective.[521] All the major studies to date show the lowest regret rate possible for any major medical or surgical procedure.

One typical study of nearly 2,000 teens found only 1.4% went off blockers or hormones.[522] Sixteen other studies have found similar rates.[523] A new study just published in Journal of the American Medical Association found that among 139 teens getting top surgery the regret rate was exactly *zero,* and the *median* satisfaction score out of a possible five was... five.[524]

So much for the specter of "irreversible" decisions and "lifelong" mistakes, not to mention "detransitioning," which may be real but is only slightly more common than left-handed unicorns.[525]

Meanwhile, regret rates for teen abortions are reportedly as high as five percent. But none of these mainstream outlets is running any stories about hitting PAUSE on *that* pediatric care.[526] [527] [528] Or on the hundreds of thousands of gender-affirming surgeries provided to cisgender teens which have regret rates exponentially higher than for their transgender peers getting the same procedures.

It's another example of *transgender exceptionalism* and society's ongoing discomfort with altering one's gender.

The coverage of the generally pro-LGBTQ+ *New York Times* in particular became so egregiously lopsided and obviously manipulative of the facts, that the paper was publicly condemned by GLAAD...*and* by 12,000 o its own journalists and contributors.[529]

As PITT's unsigned Substack post crowing about hoodwinking the *New York Times* illustrated, anti-trans Christian hate groups had studied their enemy and done a lot of message testing to take advantage of media's "soft transphobia" around GAC and youth, As journalist Imara Jones documented, "They created an entire disinformation network of pseudoscientific organizations that the Times now cites."[530] [531] (Note to NYT: When hate groups like PITT brag openly about how you are publishing their lies, it's time to review editorial standards.)

Such organizations include the evangelical Christian American College of Pediatricians, with names and brands that are designed to be confused with legitimate national medical organizations while providing a patina of fake legitimacy for mainstream organizations like the Times to publish what is essentially anti-LGBTQ+ hate speech.[532]

Finally the satirical outlet, *The Onion*, published the perfect take-down of the *New York Times* patented anti-trans style in a piece appropriately titled: "It Is Journalism's Sacred Duty To Endanger The Lives of As Many Trans People As Possible:[533]

'Quentin' is a 14-year-old assigned female at birth who now identifies as male against the wishes of his parents. His transition was supported by one of his unmarried teachers,

who is not a virgin. He stole his parents' car and drove to the hospital, where a doctor immediately began performing top surgery on him. Afterward, driving home drunk from the hospital, Quentin became suicidally depressed, and he wonders now, homeless and ridden with gonorrhea, if transitioning was a mistake...

As one Texas mom explains, "[W]hile the left still isn't sure what to say about transkids' and care, groups like Heritage and APP are investing a small fortune in identifying what issues were most vulnerable. No one is filling in the void of what it means to be a transkid except the right." And the right deploys an armory of well-honed conspiracy theories, fake hysteria, and fabricated backed by mocked-up professional organizations which—as PITT's Substack post showed—are no longer confined to obscure early morning talk shows and AM radio stations but now picked up by mainstream media and disseminated to a national audience at unheard of scale.[534] [535] [536]

As information warfare, it's a devastating for trans kids.

The broader political progression which white Christian nationalists have put into motion against the LGBTQ+ community is now clear. "Saving girls' sports" segued into saving transkids from "mutilation" and "castration," which segued into saving children from sexualization by gay drag shows; which segued into "Don't' Say Gay" laws forbidding any mention of homosexuality in schoolrooms or public libraries, which proceeded to the War's inevitable conclusion—the hoary canard that gay people are all groomers and pedos after young kids. We have returned, yet again, to Anita Bryant and Save Our Kids, except this time with transgender kids leading the way. In the coming 24 months after Texas, a Michigan library would close over its refusal to remove several award-wining LGBTQ+ books; a New Hampshire drag show would be disrupted by "Sieg Heil!" changing neo-Nazis; and a 66-year-old California store owner would be gunned down because she was displaying a large rainbow flag.[537] [538] [539]

This is what civil society has unleashed through its ambivalence and inaction on trans kids. Because underneath, attacks on trans people are always attacks on homosexuality.

Back in Texas, the Supreme Court crushes Younger's last appeal to stop Georgulas from leaving with Luna and moving out of state by 8-to-1. However, applying the kind of tormented logic which appears to be its judicial calling card, justices also note confidently that Georgulas is still subject to Texas' orders banning her from giving Luna medical care—a confidence that would presumably be unshaking if she announced she was becoming an astronaut and moving with Luna to the moon.

Granted permission to go, that December 2022 Georgulas leaves Texas immediately with her four children for California. Her life savings are gone, depleted by moving, protracted custody battles, and Younger's relentless social media attacks, which allegedly helped force the closing of her practice.[540] A GoFundMe attracts just $2,100—not even a shadow of the quarter million Younger reportedly reaped for his "Save James" campaign.[541] [542] Ironically, for all the things Younger had allegedly lied about regarding his business prowess, the one thing he'd found undeniable financial success at was monetizing attacks on his wife and their transgender daughter.

Ximena Lopez and GENECIS are still open and accepting patients. The injunction issued by Judge Bellan is part of a larger lawsuit that Lopez has filed in federal court which is still pending.[543] If successful, Lopez's lawsuit would set a precedent for pediatric gender care statewide. As she explained to me, "I'm exhausted fighting what feels like the whole state government—but if we can win this case, it will be much bigger than me or even GENECIS."[544]

In her exhaustion she is hardly alone. I interviewed many parents who were also drained and frustrated, having testified repeatedly in a running five-year battle with their own governments. Video of hearings would show hearing rooms packed with hundreds of local families waiting their turn to testify against anti-trans bills which they knew their legislatures were going to pass anyway.

But still they came.

On a personal note, I've been on hormones continuously since my transition in 1978. But after the ordinarily obedient Florida legislature twice refused to pass an anti-care bill, DeSantis took a page from Abbott's playbook and simply stacked his State Medical Board with anti-care appointees.

The newly appointed Surgeon General, Joseph Ladapo, was born in Nigeria and earned both an MD *and* a PhD from Harvard. Despite this, Ladapo has reportedly continued to promote fake treatments and falsified data showing COVID vaccines are dangerous. They are not.[545] [546] [547]

In other words, he appears strangely detached from science for an MD/ PhD and thus perfect for the task at hand.

The newly-stocked Board under his leadership manipulates data on trans care, which it commissions from a Christian fundamentalist hate group and an evangelical consultant who advocates for anti-gay "conversion therapy."[548] The Board uses this pretext to rule that Florida doctors providing care will lose their state licenses. So my doctor can no longer prescribe for me the medication I've taken without interruption or complication for nearly half a century.[549]

To avoid being forced into the hot flashes and night sweats of menopause at age 71, I planned to start flying to nearby Colombia to restock—where hormones (which are totally safe) are both cheap and available over-the-counter without prescription.[550]

As Erin Reed would put it, "Where we are in 2023 on transgender kids is where were gay marriage was in 2003. When Hawaii and Massachusetts legalized gay marriage, almost overnight, 30 states passed constitutional amendments banning it. It looked bleak. and it was: the damage was done for the next 10 years. But then look where we are today." Sometimes bleak is what civil rights progress looks like, ugly and cruel at the beginning of the curve. But we are only in the early stages. The battle for trans rights is here to stay, as are transgender people, and transgender youth.

We may be vulnerable and wounded, but while we are down, we will not go quietly.

As the Florida Medical Boards took public testimony before its inevitable vote to ban care, a transgender man would approach the podium slowly to testify for his allotted two-and-a-half minutes. He had been nervous and unsure. But as 25-year-old Lindsay Spero stands at the podium, looking at the board, he suddenly finds his voice.

"I could stand here and tell you about the times that I tried to end my life because I didn't have access to gender-affirming care, but I know you don't care. I see you sneering at us while we come here and talk to you. Instead, I'm going to take the rest of my time to demonstrate the sacred and weekly ritual of my shot in front of you and this body." Spero then injects himself under the skin of his stomach just as he does every day with a syringe of testosterone.

And then, as the crowd behind him rises in solidarity, erupting into cheers, Spero raises his fist and shouts at the Board, "Trans liberation today! Tomorrow! Forever!"[551]

Appendices

Appendix A

Of the 19 states that passed anti-trans bills:[552] [553]

Year	Bills	% Change	Abortion[554]	Voter Suppression[555]
2018	19			
2019	25	+31%		
2020	60	+140%	236[556]	
2021	131	+118%	663[557]	165[558]
2022	155	+18%	563[559]	250[560]
2023	@550	+214%	@600[561]	150[562]

Appendix B

From Komodo Health's in-depth study conducted for Reuters News of 330m patient records during the pivotal five-year period when the War on Trans youth takes off—2017 through 2021—on the rates of care being given to transgender youth.[563]

- A total of 121,882 young people ages 6 to 17 are diagnosed as transgender, that is, with *gender dysphoria*.[564]

  - 2017:   15,172
  - 2018:   18,321   +21%
  - 2019:   21,375   +17%
  - 2020:   24,847   +16%
  - 2021:   42,167   +70%

Overall rate of growth from 2017 to 2021 is 178%.

- Of the total treated, 17,683 start either puberty blocker or hormones (mostly hormones), broken down as follows:

  - 4,780 puberty blockers
  - 14,726 hormone treatment[565]

- Puberty blockers by year (new patients)
  - 2017   633
  - 2018   759
  - 2019   897
  - 2020   1,101
  - 2021   1,390

- Hormone treatment by year (new patients)
  - 2017   1,905
  - 2018   2,391
  - 2019   3,036
  - 2020   3,163
  - 2021   4,231

- Puberty blockers and hormone treatment (combined)

2017	633	2,538	
2018	759	3,150	24%
2019	897	3,933	25%
2020	1,101	4,254	8%
2021	1,390	5,621	32%

Overall rate of growth from 2017 to 2021 is 121%.

Komodo's figures do not include those young people who access care outside of standard medical systems (such as getting street hormones). More importantly they don't and can't count for the large number of children from families that are indifferent or actually hostile to their being trans, and who thus never come to the attention of a medical professional. Although the debate around care centers entirely on the families providing it, a 2023 Washington Post/KFF poll of transgender adults found that one in three are in from families that are "unsupportive." [566] [567] [568]

Tellingly, even with the number of young people being diagnosed and/or given blockers or hormones doubling and tripling, the small number of top surgeries—rarely recommended for minors and generally outside the Standards of Care except for older teens—remains both stable and a fraction of overall diagnoses. This is a sign that despite attacks on pediatricians for reflexively providing over-treatment of transteens, those delivering care are actually being quite careful, conservative, and responsible (Komodo only provides data for years 2019 – 2021):

- o 2019   238
- o 2020   256
- o 2021   282
- o Over the same three years, Komodo found just 56 bottom surgeries, about 19 per year—hardly the numbers one would expect from all the right-wing hysteria about it. Similarly, out of 121,882 minors diagnosed with gender dysphoria from 2017 to 2021, fewer than 15%, (about 3,500 per year) got blockers or hormones.

Appendix C

Exact figures are hard to come by, but below is a list of the states which had implemented bans through law or policy by early 2023 with their estimated population of transgender teens age 13-17, according to the Williams Institute's 2022 report, "How Many Adults and Youth Identify as Transgender in the United States?"[569]

Arizona	7,300
Arkansas	1,800
Idaho	1,000
Indiana	4,100
Iowa	2,100
Kentucky	2,000
Missouri	2,900
South Dakota	500
Tennessee	3,100
Texas	29,800
Utah	2,100
West Virginia	700
TOTAL	57,400

The Institute also estimated that that there are more than 100,000 trans teens living in the South, more than in any other region.

About the Author

Riki Wilchins has 25 years of writing, advocacy, and research on gender and trans issues. She is a founder of the first national transgender advocacy group, GenderPAC, as well as the direct action group The Transexual Menace [sic]. Riki is the author of seven books on gender theory and politics, and her writing has appeared in popular media outlets *The Village Voice and Social Text*, peer review publications such as *The Journal of Research on Adolescence* and *The Journal of Homosexuality*, and also her own recurring blog at Medium.com/@rikiwilchins. She has conducted gender trainings for institutions including the White House, CDC, and the HHS Office on Women's Health. Riki's work has been profiled by *The New York Times*. *TIME* magazine selected Riki among "100 Civic Innovators for the 21st Century." She lives in sunny South Beach with her partner, one daughter, two dogs, and three tennis racquets.

Footnotes

[1] https://www.washingtonpost.com/dc-md-va/2023/03/23/takeaways-post-kff-survey/

[2] There are also some in the community who are trying to move away from "trans woman" (which implies a particular kind of individual) to using "trans woman" or "transgender woman" (which implies that all in the category *are* women, but these are a particular *kind of* woman). However, I have tended to use all such terms interchangeably. The same goes for "trans man," "trans man," and "transgender man."

[3] https://www.washingtonpost.com/dc-md-va/2023/03/23/takeaways-post-kff-survey/

[4] One nonbinary writer described these binary-gendered body types: as "the intense sexual dimorphism of large breasts on soft-faced, hairless women, and heavy musculature on stubbly men with chiseled jaws." See: https://www.huffingtonpost.co.uk/entry/non-binary-desirability_uk_5c07fffee4b0bf813ef36910?utm_source=pocket_saves

[5] Brooke Migdon, "Trump vows to punish doctors, hospitals that provide gender-affirming care to transgender minors," The Hill, April 8, 2022, https://thehill.com/homenews/3839471-trump-vows-to-punish-doctors-hospitals-that-provide-gender-affirming-care-to-transgender-minors/.

[6] Erin Reed, "National Trans Bans? Both Trump and DeSantis Advocate Anti-Trans Policies On Same Day," Erin in the Morning, February 2, 2021, https://erininthemorn.substack.com/p/national-trans-bans-both-trump-and.

[7] Priya Krishnakumar, "This record-breaking year for anti-transgender legislation would affect minors the most," CNN, April 15, 2021, https://www.cnn.com/2021/04/15/politics/anti-transgender-legislation-2021/index.html.

[8] Transgender Legislation Tracker, "2022 State Bills," accessed April 7, 2023, https://translegislation.com/bills/2022.

[9] Brooke Migdon, "Here are the States Planning to Restrict Gender-Affirming Care Next Year," The Hill, December 21, 2021, https://thehill.com/changing-america/respect/diversity-inclusion/3789757-here-are-the-states-planning-to-restrict-gender-affirming-care-next-year/.

[10] According to Human Rights Watch, Tennessee would have the dark honor for the earliest filing for 2023—a bill to ban affirming care for youth filed on Nov 4, 2022, the day following the midterm elections. It was such an urgent matter that it was passed in the opening legislative rush of 2023, just three months after it was introduced. See: https://www.hrw.org /news/2022/11/18/us-state-readies-first-anti-transgender-bill-2023

[11] Jody L. Herman, Andrew R. Flores, and Kathryn K. O'Neill, "How Many Adults and Youth Identify as Transgender in the United States," Williams Institute, June 2022, https://williamsinstitute.law.ucla.edu/wp-content/uploads/Trans-Pop-Update-Jun-2022.pdf.

[12] Drag Story Hour. "Home | Drag Story Hour," n.d. https://www.dragstoryhour.org/.

[13] Gloria Oladipo, "Tennessee Governor to Ban Drag Shows – despite Photo of Him Dressed in Drag." *The Guardian*, February 28, 2023. https://www.theguardian.com/us-news/2023/feb/28/tennessee-governor-ban-drag-shows-photo-bill-lee?CMP=Share_iOSApp_Other.

[14] Livia Albeck-Ripka, "Tennessee Bans Drag Shows on Public Property." *The New York Times*, March 3, 2023. https://www.nytimes.com/2023/03/02/us/tennessee-bans-drag-shows.html.

[15] The Tennessee Holler. "UPDATE — INBOX: NASHVILLE Folks Tell Us They Took down the NAZI SIGN Hung on the Chestnut St. Bridge, Which Thanked @GovBillLee for 'Tirelessly Working to Fight Trannies and Fags' Adding 'We Must Secure a Future for White Children'. How Proud You

Must Be, Guv." *Twitter.Com*, March 2, 2023. https://twitter.com/TheTNHoller/status/1631336046016315393.

[16] https://www.usatoday.com/story/news/politics/2023/02/24/tennessee-ban-gender-affirming-care-minors/11337522002/

[17] https://www.reuters.com/world/us/tennessee-takes-lead-republican-effort-restrict-drag-shows-2023-02-23/

[18] The anti-drag law was struck down just months later by a federal judge. See: https://www.commercialappeal.com/story/news/local/2023/06/03/tennessees-unconstitutional-drag-ban-struck-down-by-federal-judge/70281619007/)

[19] https://www.city-journal.org/the-real-story-behind-drag-queen-story-hour

[20] https://www.washingtonpost.com/education/2021/06/19/critical-race-theory-rufo-republicans/

[21] https://twitter.com/realchrisrufo/status/1537807543895998464?lang=en

[22] https://www.washingtonpost.com/lifestyle/2022/10/14/anti-trans-bills/

[23] Wilchins, Riki & Souchere, Chloe, Analysis of ACLU Transgender legislation, unpublished raw data, 2023 https://www.aclu.org/legislative-attacks-on-lgbtq-rights

[24] Jo Yurcaba, "North Dakota advances record-setting 10 anti-LGBTQ bills in one day, advocates say," NBC News, February 25, 2023, https://www.nbcnews.com/nbc-out/out-politics-and-policy/north-dakota-advances-record-setting-10-anti-lgbtq-bills-one-day-advoc-rcna78311.

[25] https://williamsinstitute.law.ucla.edu/publications/trans-adults-united-states/

[26] According to Rolling Stone, it was the ultra-conservative, corporate front ALEC (American Legislative Exchange Council) which pioneered the Republican tactic of promoting national political change by pushing carbon-copy bills through numerous state legislatures simultaneously. See:Tim Dickinson, "The Christian Nationalist Machine Turning Hate Into Law," Rolling Stone, October 21, 2021, https://www.rollingstone.com/politics/politics-features/christian-nationalists-national-association-christian-lawmakers-1234684542/. In this case, it also makes mounting any kind

of organized resistance or boycott difficult, since it's impossible to boycott half of America.

[27] As attorney Alejandra Caraballo would point out the evangelical Christian right uses the same talking points for GAC and medication abortion: "1. Not FDA approved for most uses (off label prescribing) 2. Side effects are horrific, increases suicide, strokes etc. 3. You'll regret it. 4. Teens can't consent." https://twitter.com/Esqueer_/status/1670918653632471040

[28] Erin in the Morning, "Utah, Mississippi, and Florida Race To Ban Care For TransYouth," January 20, End of the Rainbow Podcast, podcast audio, 22:34, https://www.podbean.com/ew/pb-icf8u-107a1c9.

[29] "Transgender Rights & Legislation," TransLegislation.com, accessed April 7, 2023, https://translegislation.com/learn.

[30] Grace Eliza Goodwin, "Utah just banned gender-affirming healthcare for transgender kids. These 21 other states are considering similar bills in 2023," Insider, January 27, 2023, https://www.insider.com/states-considering-bills-ban-gender-affirming-healthcare-transgender-youth-2023-1.

[31] "Kentucky House Bill 470," LegiScan, accessed April 7, 2023, https://legiscan.com/KY/bill/HB470/2023.

[32] Bizarrely, HB 470 would also "require that corporate income relating to the provision of gender transition services to a person under age 18 years be added to net income," apparently to ensure that any corporation providing any care-related services couldn't take it as an expense, but would have to pay taxes on it.

[33] Olivia Krauth, "New, sweeping anti-trans bill being fast-tracked in Kentucky legislature," The Courier-Journal, February 22, 2023, https://www.courier-journal.com/story/news/politics/2023/02/22/kentucky-lawmakers-launch-new-bill-on-transgender-kids-teacher-rules/69931156007/.

[34] Jennifer Henderson Decker, "About Jennifer Henderson Decker," Jennifer Henderson Decker State Representative, accessed April 2023, https://jenniferhensondecker.com/about.

[35] Beatrice Adler-Bolton, "Imagine What We'll Build for One Another: An Interview with Jules Gill-Peterson," The New Inquiry, May 28, 2021, https://thenewinquiry.com/imagine-

what-well-build-for-one-another-an-interview-with-jules-gill-peterson/?utm_source=pocket_mylist.

[36] In anti-colonial studies also called *necropolitics*. See: "Necropolitics," Wikipedia, last modified March 15, 2023, https://en.wikipedia.org/wiki/Necropolitics.

[37] "Student Preparticipation Physical Evaluation," Florida High School Athletic Association, accessed April 2023, https://fhsaa.com/documents/2020/3/26/el02_physical_2.pdf.

[38] The form did remain online for school athletic departments to download and use if they wanted—for instance if they had a suspected transgender athlete.

[39] Trisha Ahmed, "North Dakota Considers $1,500 Fine for Using Pronouns Other Than Those Assigned at Birth," PBS NewsHour, January 17, 2022, https://www.pbs.org/newshour/nation/north-dakota-considers-1500-fine-for-using-pronouns-other-than-those-assigned-at-birth.

[40] "Litter boxes in schools hoax," Wikipedia, accessed April 7, 2023, https://en.wikipedia.org/wiki/Litter_boxes_in_schools_hoax.

[41] Lavanya VJ, "Bruce Bostelman: Nebraska lawmaker is trolled for spreading a debunked theory about furries," MEAWW, accessed April 7, 2023, https://meaww.com/nebraska-lawmaker-is-trolled-for-spreading-a-debunked-theory-about-furries.

[42] Jude Dry, "'South Park': A Brief History of the Show's Most Transphobic Episodes," IndieWire, November 3, 2019, https://www.indiewire.com/2019/11/south-park-trans-transphobic-lgbt-1202190642/.

[43] Tyler kingkade, Ben Goggin, Ben Collins, and Brandy Zadrozny, "How an urban myth about litter boxes in schools became a GOP talking point," NBC News, October 14, 2022, https://www.nbcnews.com/tech/misinformation/urban-myth-litter-boxes-schools-became-gop-talking-point-rcna51439.

[44] Chisholm, Johanna. "Colorado Schools Forced to Tell GOP Candidate to Stop Saying Students Identify as Cats." The Independent, October 5, 2022. https://www.independent.co.uk/news/world/americas/us-politics/heidi-ganahl-colorado-furries-identify-b2196410.html

[45] Some nasty rhetorical work is being compressed into this brief quote: that supporting transstudents means allowing students to change genders every week, that this then equates with their peeing in litterboxes, and both of these therefore equal going insane.

[46] The panic about school students identifying as cats and dogs would even spread to the UK, and the Daily Mail would warn the public about outbreaks of furries. See: https://www.the guardian.com/education/2023/jun/23/child-identifying-as-cat-controversy-from-a-tiktok-video-to-media-frenzy?CMP= Share_AndroidApp_Other

[47] "Tyler Perry's Ultimate Thanksgiving Playlist," YouTube video, posted by O, The Oprah Magazine, November 21, 2019, https://www.youtube.com/watch?v=dnaRIXObuT8 (at minute 1:20).

[48] Patterson, Thom. "Inside the Misunderstood Culture of Furries." CNN, November 14, 2018. https://www.cnn.com/2018/11/14/us/furries-culture/index.html.

[49] Tyler Kingkade, Twitter post, February 14, 2022, 5:14 PM, https://twitter.com/tylerkingkade/status/1580954470372212736.

[50] Erin Reed, "Bill Cites Litterbox Hoax To Ban TransKids From Bathrooms In North Dakota," Erin in the Morning, January 22, 2023.

[51] Eventually, and perhaps inevitably, the litterbox hoax would be picked up and promoted as "news" on Fox. See: https://twitter.com/LisPower1/status/1694756884790521988

[52] Jeremy W. Peters "Why Transgender Girls Are Suddenly the G.O.P.'s Culture-War Focus." The New York Times, March 29, 2021. https://www.nytimes.com/2021/03/29/us/politics/trans gender-girls-sports.html.

[53] Migdon, Brooke. "The Hill." The Hill, February 1, 2023. https://thehill.com/homenews/3839471-trump-vows-to-punish-doctors-hospitals-that-provide-gender-affirming-care-to-transgender-minors/.

[54] https://www.nytimes.com/2023/04/16/us/politics/transgender-conservative-campaign.html

[55] Jeremy W. Peters "Why Transgender Girls Are Suddenly the G.O.P.'s Culture-War Focus." The New York Times, March 29, 2021.

https://www.nytimes.com/2021/03/29/us/politics/trans gender-girls-sports.html.

[56] Jeremy W. Peters "Why Transgender Girls Are Suddenly the G.O.P.'s Culture-War Focus." The New York Times, March 29, 2021. https://www.nytimes.com/2021/03/29/us/politics/trans gender-girls-sports.html.

[57] https://www.weekendreading.net/p/hiding-in-plain-sight-the-sources

[58] Francesca D'Annunzio, Lauren Irwin, and Janae Bradford. "Christian nationalism is on the rise, but it's difficult to quantify its financial influence in elections." Society of American Business Editors and Writers. December 12, 2022. https://businessjournalism.org/2022/12/christian-nationalism/.

[59] Peter Smith and Deepa Bharath. "Christian nationalism on the rise in some GOP campaigns." AP News. November 23, 2022. https://apnews.com/article/2022-midterm-elections-pennsylvania-religion-nationalism-8bf7a6115725f50 8a37ef944333bc145.

[60] Chrissy Stroop, "Christian nationalism is authentically Christian — and according to a new poll most white evangelicals are supporters," Religion Dispatches, February 9, 2023, https://religiondispatches.org/christian-nationalism-is-authentically-christian-and-according-to-a-new-poll-most-white-evangelicals-are-supporters/.

[61] https://www.cnn.com/2022/07/24/us/white-christian-nationalism-blake-cec/index.html

[62] https://religiondispatches.org/the-fake-christian-deflection-and-contrarian-concern-trolling-how-not-to-write-about-evangelical-authoritarianism/

[63] https://www.weekendreading.net/p/hiding-in-plain-sight-the-sources

[64] Philip S. Gorski and Samuel L. Pery, The Flag and the Cross: A Christian Nationalism and American Democracy, Oxford University Press, 2020, https://read.amazon.com/sample/ B09SGJSQRP?f=1&r=89287537&sid=135-0039282-3750410&rid=&cid=A277P59FPQSCBI&clientId=kfw&l=e n_US&asin=B09SGJSQRP&revisionId=89287537&format= 1&depth=1.

[65] "Quick to Listen: What Is Christian Nationalism?" podcast, Christianity Today, January 21, 2021, https://www.christianitytoday.com/ct/podcasts/quick-to-listen/christian-nationalism-capitol-riots-trump-podcast.html.

[66] Kelefa Sanneh, "How Christian Is Christian Nationalism?" The New Yorker, April 3, 2023, https://www.newyorker.com/magazine/2023/04/03/how-christian-is-christian-nationalism.

[67] https://www.nytimes.com/2023/07/30/opinion/state-of-evangelical-america.html

[68] Alabama, Arizona Arkansas, Florida, Kentucky, Louisiana, Mississippi, Missouri, Ohio, Oklahoma, South Dakota, Tennessee, Texas, West Virginia, and Wisconsin

[69] https://www.motherjones.com/politics/2023/03/anti-trans-transgender-health-care-ban-legislation-bill-minors-children-lgbtq/?utm_source=substack&utm_medium=email

[70] The figures in this paragraph and the following are from our analysis of the ACLU's anti-LGBTQ+ legislative data and PPRI's 2020 Census of American Religion

[71] "Lethal fetal abnormality," You.com, accessed April 7, 2023, https://you.com/search?q=lethal+fetal+abnormality&tbm=youchat&cid=c0_c8de2961-004a-4076-a15b-318b5a1e7e0e.

[72] The anti-abortion bill was apparently so draconian, that shortly after passage, Republican legislators began exploring ways amendments that would make its provisions less damaging

[73] Samuel Stebbins. "States With the Most Active Hate Groups Per Person." 24/7 Wall St., January 14, 2023, https://247wallst.com/ special-report/2023/01/14/states-with-the-most-active-hate-groups-per-person/2/.

[74] Alejandra O'Connel-Domenech. "This US State Is Home to the Most Hate Groups." The Hill, February 24, 2022, https://thehill.com/changing-america/respect/equality/588638-this-us-state-is-home-to-the-most-hate-groups/.

[75] https://abcnews.go.com/Politics/dozen-state-laws-shift-power-elections-partisan-entities/story?id=79408455

[76] Arizona, Arkansas, Georgia, Florida, Kansas, Kentucky, Montana, and Texas

[77] https://www.npr.org/2021/08/13/1026588142/map-see-which-states-have-restricted-voter-access-and-which-states-have-expanded

[78] Arizona, Arkansas, Florida, Georgia, Iowa, Kansas, Montana, Texas, and Wyoming

[79] For instance, majorities of Republicans now believe that Obama was not born in America and that Trump did not try to overthrow the 2020 election.

[80] For instance, APP board chair, Sean Fieler and reportedly its largest donor, is also on the board of the leading anti-abortion PAC, Susan B. Anthony List. The List, along with APP, have jointly been leading forces behind the launch of the so-called Election Transparency Initiative" a nationwide GOP voter suppression effort. Election Transparency Initiative is also tied to Richard Uihlein, reportedly one of the largest single donors to APP PAC, who also funds another voter suppression effort known as VoterRef. See: https://www.nytimes.com/2023/05/08/us/politics/voting-laws-restrictions-republicans.html
https://www.ncronline.org/news/editorial/editorial-money-shapes-us-catholic-narrative
https://www.ncronline.org/opinion/guest-voices/wealthy-conservative-catholics-are-new-us-magisterium

[81] https://www.cnn.com/2023/10/31/politics/mike-johnson-donald-trump-religious-right/index.html

[82] Jay Rochlin, "The KKK is alive and well in the Midwest, and it helped fuel the Jan. 6 insurrection," The Washington Post, April 3, 2023, https://www.washingtonpost.com/opinions/2023/04/03/kkk-midwest-jan6-indiana/.

[83] https://www.loc.gov/classroom-materials/united-states-history-primary-source-timeline/colonial-settlement-1600-1763/virginia-relations-with-native-americans/

[84] Evangelicalism is also found in Latin America, Africa, and Asia where it may lack the U.S.'s MAGA-political fervors.

[85] By many definitions, Pentecostals could be considered evangelicals, although there has historically also been significant antagonism between Pentecostals—with their emphasis on direct personal experience of the Holy Spirit and "speaking in tongues"—and other evangelical sects. In fact, some scholars draw a distinction between Pentecostals and similar charismatic sects from fundamentalism.

[86] Yonat Shimron, "29% of Americans and 38% of Latter-day Saints are Christian nationalists," The Salt Lake Tribune,

February 10, 2023, https://www.sltrib.com/religion/2023/02/10/29-americans-38-latter-day/.

[87] https://www.prri.org/research/findings-from-the-2022-american-values-atlas/

[88] Although they were still the only denominations besides Hispanic Protestants and Jehovah's Witnesses in which majority were opposed to gay marriage. Similarly, they still had the lowest level of support for non-discrimination protections of any except Jehovah's Witnesses (51%).

[89] https://www.prri.org/research/a-christian-nation-understanding-the-threat-of-christian-nationalism-to-american-democracy-and-culture/

[90] Andrew L. Whitehead and Samuel L. Perry, Taking America Back for God: Christian Nationalism in the United States, (Oxford University Press, 2020), https://www.amazon.com/Taking-America-Back-God-Nationalism/dp/B088N6M83F/ref=sr_1_1?crid=1LWJRJPIEJV6A&keywords=whitehead+and+perry&qid=1680353509&sprefix=whitehead+and+perry%2Caps%2C107&sr=8-1.

[91] "Quick to Listen: What Is Christian Nationalism?" podcast, Christianity Today. https://www.christianitytoday.com/ct/podcasts/quick-to-listen/christian-nationalism-capitol-riots-trump-podcast.html

[92] https://www.prri.org/research/threats-to-american-democracy-ahead-of-an-unprecedented-presidential-election/

[93] https://www.lsu.edu/research/news/2020/1109-unchurched.php

[94] https://religiondispatches.org/the-fake-christian-deflection-and-contrarian-concern-trolling-how-not-to-write-about-evangelical-authoritarianism/

[95] https://newrepublic.com/article/156415/faith-militant

[96] https://www.nytimes.com/2022/07/08/us/christian-nationalism-politicians.html
https://www.propublica.org/article/voter-ref-foundation

[97] https://www.cnn.com/2022/07/24/us/white-christian-nationalism-blake-cec/index.html

[98] This helps account for the weird cult of personality it has erected around Trump aggressive authoritarianism and its attraction to his sense of nativist rage and grievance. See: Yonat Shimron, "A Third of Americans Are Christian

Nationalists, and Most Are White Evangelicals," Religion News Service, February 8, 2023, https://religionnews.com/2023/02/08/a-third-of-americans-are-christian-nationalists-and-most-are-white-evangelicals/.

[99] https://www.nytimes.com/2023/05/15/opinion/christian-nationalism-election-2024.html

[100] https://newrepublic.com/article/156415/faith-militant

[101] Yonat Shimron, "A Third of Americans Are Christian Nationalists, and Most Are White Evangelicals," Religion News Service, February 8, 2023, https://religionnews.com/2023/02/08/a-third-of-americans-are-christian-nationalists-and-most-are-white-evangelicals/.

[102] [ibid] Mark Galli and Morgan Lee, "The Capitol Riot Revealed Christian Nationalism's Deep Roots," Quick to Listen (podcast), Christianity Today, January 14, 2021, https://www.christianitytoday.com/ct/podcasts/quick-to-listen/christian-nationalism-capitol

[103] We see it already in how a Supreme Court, dominated by extreme-right Catholic justices, is imposing their own fundamentally religious vision on civil and reproductive rights, upending one long-established and widely-accepted precedent after another. (Neil Gorsuch was raised Catholic, but reportedly not attends church as an Episcopalian.) We also see it in how the rightwing judicial group The Federalist Society—which selects federal court nominees for Republican presidents—is has begun focusing on the developing legal tools to lock in what Harvard's Theda Skocpol calls "minority authoritarianism," which will enable GOP minorities to legally neuter majority-elected executives at every level (urban mayors and D.A.s, Democratic governors, etc.) See: https://www.nytimes.com/2023/04/12/opinion/republican-party-intrusive-government.html

[104] Jody L. Herman, Andrew R. Flores, and Kathryn K. O'Neill, "How Many Adults and Youth Identify as Transgender in the United States," Williams Institute, June 2022, https://williams institute.law.ucla.edu/wp-content/uploads/Trans-Pop-Update-Jun-2022.pdf.

[105] Reed, E. (2023, January 11). It Was Never About Sports: The Strategy Of The Anti-Trans Right. *Erin in the Morning*.

https://erininthemorn.substack.com/p/it-was-never-about-sports-the-strategy

[106] Julie Kliegman. Sports Illustrated, June 30, 2020, https://www.si.com/sports-illustrated/2020/06/30/idaho-transgender-ban-fighting-back?utm_source=substack&utm_medium=email.

[107] Sara Murray. "Republicans Build Momentum as They Drive Anti-LGBTQ Legislation Nationwide." WRAL, April 22, 2022, https://www.wral.com/republicans-build-momentum-as-they-drive-anti-lgbtq-legislation-nationwide/20247265/?utm_source=substack&utm_medium=email.

[108] Sara Murray. "Republicans build momentum as they drive anti-LGBTQ+ legislation nationwide." CNN, April 22, 2022, https://www.cnn.com/2022/04/22/politics/republicans-anti-lgbtq-legislation/index.html?utm_source=substack&utm_medium=email.

[109] Maggie Astor. "G.O.P. State Lawmakers Push a Growing Wave of Anti-Transgender Bills." The New York Times, January 30, 2023. https://www.nytimes.com/2023/01/25/us/politics/trans gender-laws-republicans.html.

[110] ADF is known for consistently taking the most extreme anti-LGBTQ+ position possible on nearly every issue. It is also active abroad, fighting to keep "same-sex sodomy" criminalized in Belize, India, Jamaica, and Uganda; against transgender rights in France, Bulgaria, Russia, in Macedonia; and supporting laws in the 20+ countries which still require compulsory sterilization of transgender people to legally change their sex (a barbarity also inflicted by such liberal countries as France, The Netherlands, and Sweden until fairly recently). It has also reportedly been a major supporter of the new Uganda law which would punish "aggravated homosexuality" with the death penalty. See: https://www.reuters.com/graphics/UGANDA-LGBT/movakykrjva/

[111] Saul, Stephanie, and Danny Hakim. "The Most Powerful Conservative Couple You've Never Heard Of." The New York Times, June 7, 2018. https://www.nytimes.com/2018/06/07/us/politics/liz-dick-uihlein-republican-donors.html.

[112] Miranda Blue, "Meet Sean Fieler, the Hedge Fund Manager Running Anti-Choice 'Talking Fetus' Ads in New York."

Right Wing Watch, March 10, 2014, https://www.rightwing
watch.org/post/meet-sean-fieler-the-hedge-fund-manager-
running-anti-choice-talking-fetus-ads-in-new-york/.

[113] Paul Blumenthal, "Sean Fieler Is Out And Proud About His Anti-
Gay Marriage Donations Even As The Country's Opinion
Shifts," HuffPost, June 5, 2015, https://www.huffpost.com/
entry/sean-fieler-gay-marriage_n_7511614.

[114] https://www.cnn.com/2023/02/11/us/he-gets-us-super-bowl-
commercials-cec/index.html

[115] SourceWatch, "Alliance Defending Freedom," https://www.
sourcewatch.org/index.php/Alliance_Defending_Freedom#F
unding.

[116] According to ADF's 2021 financials, the last year for which
data is available.

[117] https://www.hobbylobby.com/about-us/our-story

[118] Philip Rucker, "Mitt Romney Says 'Corporations Are
People.'" *Washington Post*, August 11, 2011. https://www.
washingtonpost.com/politics/mitt-romney-says-corporations-
are-people/2011/08/11/gIQABwZ38I_story.html.

[119] https://www.nytimes.com/2014/07/01/us/hobby-lobby-case-
supreme-court-contraception.html

[120] https://www.cincinnati.com/story/news/2016/06/23/who-pays-
new-ark-taxpayers/85481082/

[121] https://www.newyorker.com/news/news-desk/zooey-zephyr-
and-the-illiberal-decorum-of-montanas-christian-right

[122] Evan Vorpahl, "Another Anti-Choice Front Group Fueled By
Dick Uihlein Jumps Into Race," March 17, 2023,
https://truenorthresearch.org/2023/03/another-anti-choice-
front-group-fueled-by-dick-uihlein-jumps-into-race/.

[123] Phoebe Petrovic, "Anti-trans ads favoring Wisconsin Supreme
Court candidate Daniel Kelly peddle fear, false info,"
Wisconsin Watch, March 31, 2023, https://wisconsinwatch.
org/2023/03/wisconsin-supreme-court-daniel-kelly-anti-
trans-ads/?utm_source=substack&utm_medium=email.

[124] For example, in the campaign for the pivotal deciding seat on
Wisconsin's Supreme Court, APP PAC would reportedly
would spend $700k to blanket the state with lurid text
message and video ads claiming that the Democratic

candidate supported "woke" schools that were "transing" children behind parents' backs.

[125] This is part of the motto of Ralph Reed's Christian Coalition: "Think like Jesus, vote like Jefferson, and fight like David."

[126] Second Coming: The Strategies of the New Christian Right Mark J. Rozell, Clyde Wilcox Political Science Quarterly, Vol. 111, No. 2 (Summer, 1996), pp. 271-294 https://www.jstor.org/stable/2152322
https://doi.org/10.2307/2152322

[127] Religious Coalitions in the New Christian Right, Clyde Wilcox, Mark J. Rozell and Roland Gunn Social Science Quarterly, Vol. 77, No. 3 (September 1996), pp. 543-558

[128] Chrissy Stroop, "New Report: White Evangelicals Are America's Most Anti-Trans Demographic but Encouraging Data Overall," Religion Dispatches, September 30, 2021, https://religiondispatches.org/new-report-white-evangelicals-are-americas-most-anti-trans-demographic-but-encouraging-data-overall/.

[129] In many ways it was replay of the rightwing's 1950s "Lavender Scare" —the homosexual counterpart of the better-known "Red Scare" during which thousands of military and diplomatic personnel were fired and tens of thousands more investigated on suspicions of being homosexual, nearly bringing the federal government to a halt. Sen. Joe McCarthy, who had bragged to Congress that he carried a "list of 205 card-carrying Communists" in the State Department, explained that "[t]he pervert is easy prey to the blackmailer;" gloating to reporters, "If you want to be against McCarthy, boys, you've got to be either a Communist or a faggot." This was rich, since two of his main supporters in the metastasizing witch-hunt were lawyer Roy Cohn (later Trump's mentor) and feared FBI chief J. Edgar Hoover—both of whom were later found to be gay, themselves. Congress held bipartisan national TV hearings on the "problem" of homosexuality in government and President Dwight D. Eisenhower—World War II's heroic Supreme Commander and a Republican—was accused of "harboring homosexuals." In its zeal to demonstrate its Godliness, the federal government added the words "under God" to the

Pledge of Allegiance, and formally adopted "In God We
Trust" as the country's official motto. See: Robert Longley,
"Lavender Scare: The Government's Gay Witch Hunt,"
ThoughtCo, November 27, 2019,
https://www.thoughtco.com/lavender-scare-4776081
[130] Texas attorney (now judge) Phyllis Frye's annual trans law
gathering was a remarkable exception.
[131] https://www.nytimes.com/1996/09/08/us/shunning-he-and-
she-they-fight-for-respect.html
[132] The article was bizarrely titled "Shunning He and She, They
Fight for Respect." Nonbinary wasn't really around then and
in any case, none of us shunned using pronouns. But the at
least the "fighting for respect" part was accurate. Strangely
enough, their only picture showed several attendees sitting in
a subway car on our way to Lobby Day. I'm sure leaving
many Times readers puzzled over their morning coffee
wondering why we were fighting for our rights down in the
DC Metro.
[133] Prior to that, we were confined to culture or fashion sections—
usually in entertainment stories (Bond Girl actress Carolyn
Cossey being outed), literature (travel writer Jan Morris's
autobiography *Conundrum*) or some off-off-off Broadway
drag-themed play (actor Charles Busch in *Vampire Lesbians
of Sodom* and about a hundred others)—if we appeared at all.
[134] The protest group Transexual Menace [*sic*] actually picketed
Lambda over this in the summer of 1998 ("Lambda Legal to
Transsexuals, Transgender People, Drag Queens, & Butch
Lesbians: GET LOST!").
[135] The ACLU, to its everlasting credit, has always seen the trans
as a legal and civil rights issue, perhaps because it is
organized around the principle of civil rights, rather than any
particular identity.
[136] A running joke on the show was that Cpl. Klinger was dressed
in feminine clothing in the forlorn hope of being granted a
Section 8 "insanity" Army discharge which would free him
from serving in the Korean War.
[137] As Andrea Dworkin notes in her book Rightwing Women, this
was not limited to gay men: "[To rightwing women] the
lesbian was inherently monstrous, experienced almost as a

demonic sexual force hovering closer and closer… [and] threatening by her very presence a sexual order that cannot bear scrutiny or withstand challenge."

[138] Barnett Nesbit & Sorrento 2018 The Transgender Bathroom Debate

[139] Neil J Young, How the Bathroom Wars Shaped America, Politico

[140] https://sncclegacyproject.org/in-memoriam-samuel-leamon-younge-jr/?utm_source=rss&utm_medium=rss&utm_campaign=in-memoriam-samuel-leamon-younge-jr

[141] 68-year-old Marvin Segrest would be acquitted of the murder by an all-white jury.

[142] Neil J Young, How the Bathroom Wars Shaped America, Politico

[143] Notwithstanding its outrageously homophobic bias and blank acceptance of medical testimony that homosexuality is a psychiatric illness, CBS's management still considered the show *too pro-gay*, and had it re-edited so that the gay people interviewed looked more unhappy than they had been. Despite this, it was broadcast without commercials; no advertiser wanted its products associated with homosexuality, so none bought ad time on the show. See: https://en.wikipedia.org/wiki/The_Homosexuals_(CBS_Reports)

[144] https://www.thepinknews.com/2016/09/06/anti-equality-conservative-phyllis-schlafly-dies-aged-92/

[145] https://eagleforum.org/publications/psr/sept1974.html

[146] Anti-ERA forces also claimed women would be drafted into the armed forces and lose alimony in cases of divorce—both of which were untrue.

[147] https://thesocietypages.org/socimages/2015/11/10/protecting-white-women-in-the-bathroom-history/

[148] https://news.gallup.com/poll/154634/acceptance-gay-lesbian-relations-new-normal.aspx

[149] IBID https://news.gallup.com/poll/154634/acceptance-gay-lesbian-relations-new-normal.aspx

[150] https://news.gallup.com/poll/350486/record-high-support-same-sex-marriage.aspx

[151] Title VII of the 1964 Civil Rights Act forbade discrimination "because of sex."

[152]https://en.wikipedia.org/wiki/Bostock_v._Clayton_County#Intr oduction

[153] https://americanprinciplesproject.org/medi /new-app-report-exposes-origins-influence-transgender-leviathan/

[154] https://www.msnbc.com/msnbc-podcast/why-is-this-happening/discussing-fixation-anti-trans-legislation-chase-strangio-podcast-transcript-n1304130

[155] https://www.pewresearch.org/religion/2016/09/28/5-vast-majority-of-americans-know-someone-who-is-gay-fewer-know-someone-who-is-transgender/

[156] https://www.pewresearch.org/fact-tank/2022/06/07/about-5-of-young-adults-in-the-u-s-say-their-gender-is-different-from-their-sex-assigned-at-birth/

[157] https://www.thetrevorproject.org/blog/new-poll-majority-of-u-s-adults-are-comfortable-having-lgbtq-children-fewer-than-1-in-3-know-someone-who-is-transgender/

[158] In almost two decades of working in transgender rights, I've participated in dozens of meetings and conference calls with national gay rights groups. I never once heard any mention gender or gender expression except in relation to transgender people. Effeminate gay men and masculine/butch lesbians had completely ceased to exist in official discourse.

[159] This strategy of avoiding any acknowledgement of gay gender nonconformity also facilitated the coming evangelical extremist attacks on drag, which became the fulcrum of its charges that gays were "sexualizing" children.

[160] In an overwrought article in the City Journal, Christopher F. Rufo—who The New Yorker would credit with helping invent the "crisis" over Critical Race Theory,—would declare ominously: "The drag queen might appear as a comic figure, but he carries an utterly serious message: the deconstruction of sex, the reconstruction of child sexuality, and the subversion of middle-class family life. The ideology that drives this movement was born in the sex dungeons of San Francisco and incubated in the academy. It is now being transmitted, with official state support, in a number of public libraries….." https://www.city-journal.org/the-real-story-behind-drag-queen-story-hour

[161] https://www.komodohealth.com/insights/komodo-findings-point-to-rising-healthcare-needs-for-transgender-youth

[162] https://www.reuters.com/investigates/special-report/usa-transyouth-data/

[163] https://www.ncsl.org/resources/details/number-of-legislators-and-length-of-terms-in-years

[164] It was particularly rife among upper and middle-upper class families with male offspring.

[165] https://jodebloggs.wordpress.com/2015/03/19/why-was-masturbation-such-a-medical-concern-in-the-19th-century/

[166] https://www.oah.org/tah/issues/2018/november/evangelicalism-and-politics/

[167] https://www.nytimes.com/2023/04/12/opinion/republican-party-intrusive-government.html

[168] https://www.politico.com/story/2017/01/full-text-donald-trump-inauguration-speech-transcript-233907

[169] https://www.nationalreview.com/2003/05/rick-santorum-right-robert-p-george/

[170] https://www.youtube.com/watch?v=-sED4fzIV0k

[171] See: https://twitter.com/Schilling1776/status/1669394782613798936

[172] Butler's piece also included a section on TERFS, or Trans Exclusionary Radical Feminists, and their alliance with exactly these revanchist anti-women forces, for which The Guardian would come under so much pressure from TERFs that it would censor that section of the piece. https://www.huffpost.com/entry/guardian-judith-butler-interview-trans-terfs_n_6138d856e4b0f1b9706915be

[173] Far-right parties in Austria, France, Germany, India, Israel, Puerto Rico, Peru, and Romania—to name just a few—have also attacked gender ideology generally and/or LGBTQ+ people specifically as immoral and dangerous.

[174] https://www.nytimes.com/2022/03/31/world/europe/putin-jk-rowling.html

[175] In 2023, House Republicans and Russian parliament would introduce anti-care bills within a couple months of one another: the Russians to "protect Russia with its cultural and family values and traditions and to stop the infiltration of the Western anti-family ideology: and the Republicans to stop

trans members of the military. See:
https://apnews.com/article/russia-lgbt-gender-surgery-parliament-65faa0fe898e3e1996d806ba68df4d8c and
https://www.military.com/daily-news/2023/06/13/va-barred-abortions-flying-pride-flags-transgender-health-care-under-gop-bill.html

[176] https://www.splcenter.org/news/2022/06/01/poll-finds-support-great-replacement-hard-right-ideas

[177] Not that some legislators wouldn't try. According to a Feb 15th tweet by the ACLU's Chase Strangio, Oklahoma had introduced a bill which would outlaw care for transgender adults as well, and Arkansas bill would make it a crime for transperson to use the proper restroom if a minor could be present—not *was*, but *could be.*

[178] Alexa Ura. "Bathroom Fears Flush Houston Discrimination Ordinance." *The Texas Tribune*, August 7, 2018. https://www.texastribune.org/2015/11/03/houston-anti-discrimination-ordinance-early-voting/.

[179] Mark Joseph Stern, "Texas Supreme Court Rules Houston LGBT Rights Ordinance Must Be Put to a Vote—or Repealed." *Slate Magazine*, July 24, 2015. https://slate.com/human-interest/2015/07/texas-supreme-court-puts-houston-lgbt-rights-ordinance-in-danger.html.

[180] Alexa Ura. "Bathroom Fears Flush Houston Discrimination Ordinance." *The Texas Tribune*, August 7, 2018. https://www.texastribune.org/2015/11/03/houston-anti-discrimination-ordinance-early-voting/.

[181] Alexa Ura. "Bathroom Fears Flush Houston Discrimination Ordinance." *The Texas Tribune*, August 7, 2018. https://www.texastribune.org/2015/11/03/houston-anti-discrimination-ordinance-early-voting/.

[182] PRRI Staff, "The 2020 Census of American Religion - PRRI," June 2, 2022. https://www.prri.org/research/2020-census-of-american-religion/.

[183] https://www.aclu.org/cases/grimm-v-gloucester-county-school-board

[184] American Civil Liberties Union. "Grimm v. Gloucester County School Board | American Civil Liberties Union,"

October 6, 2021. https://www.aclu.org/cases/grimm-v-gloucester-county-school-board.

[185] Greg Lacour, "The Growing War Over The Restroom Thing - Charlotte Magazine." Charlotte Magazine, September 30, 2019. https://www.charlottemagazine.com/the-growing-war-over-the-restroom-thing/.

[186] https://adflegal.org/about-us/who-we-are

[187] https://www.theguardian.com/world/2023/jun/30/christian-hate-group-funding-us-anti-lgbtq-anti-abortion-organizations?CMP=Share_AndroidApp_Other

[188] https://www.newyorker.com/magazine/2023/10/09/alliance-defending-freedoms-legal-crusade

[189] ADF also successfully defended the anti-abortion in *Dobbs v. Jackson Women's Health Organization* which overturned *Roe v Wade*.

[190] https://twitter.com/GBBranstetter/status/1708939876081496496

[191] https://www.newsweek.com/jesus-super-bowl-commercial-anti-lgbt-anti-abortion-group-1780776

[192] https://www.hobbylobby.com/about-us/our-story

[193] https://www.nytimes.com/2014/07/01/us/hobby-lobby-case-supreme-court-contraception.html

[194] It was a real-life example of Mitt Romney's "Corporations are people." See: Philip Rucker, "Mitt Romney Says 'Corporations Are People.'" *Washington Post*, August 11, 2011. https://www.washingtonpost.com/politics/mitt-romney-says-corporations-are-people/2011/08/11/gIQABwZ38I_story.html.

[195] https://www.cincinnati.com/story/news/2016/06/23/who-pays-new-ark-taxpayers/85481082/

[196] https://www.nytimes.com/2020/04/05/arts/bible-museum-artifacts.html?utm_source=affiliate&utm_medium=Linkbux&utm_campaign=wizKxmN8no4&utm_content=486358&utm_term=15819104244&siteID=wizKxmN8no4-jrrdHiirm09M0.UEojAt6A&ranMID=39812&ranEAID=wizKxmN8no4&ranSiteID=wizKxmN8no4-jrrdHiirm09M0.UEojAt6A

[197] ADF consistently takes the most anti-LGBTQ+ position possible on nearly every issue, and offers to defend those attacking us pro bono. No bottom too low, ADF has fought to keep "same-sex sodomy" criminal in the US, Belize, India,

Jamaica, and Uganda; fought against transgender rights in France, Bulgaria, Russia, in Macedonia; and supported laws in the 20+ countries which still require the compulsory sterilization of transgender people before they can legally change their sex (a barbarity also inflicted by such liberal countries as France, The Netherlands, and Sweden until fairly recently).

[198] https://www.newyorker.com/news/news-desk/zooey-zephyr-and-the-illiberal-decorum-of-montanas-christian-right

[199] Camila Domonoske, "North Carolina Passes Law Blocking Measures To Protect LGBT People." *NPR*, March 24, 2016. https://www.npr.org/sections/thetwo-way/2016/03/24/471700323/north-carolina-passes-law-blocking-measures-to-protect-lgbt-people.

[200] "Public Facilities Privacy & Security Act." *Wikipedia*, January 29, 2023. https://en.wikipedia.org/wiki/Public_Facilities_Privacy_%26_Security_Act.

[201] Greg Lacour, "A Governor, an Attorney General, and a Transgender Kid - Charlotte Magazine." Charlotte Magazine, April 13, 2021. https://www.charlottemagazine.com/a-governor-an-attorney-general-and-a-transgender-kid/.

[202] Amber Phillips, "The Tumultuous History of North Carolina's Bathroom Bill, Which Is on Its Way to Repeal." *Washington Post*, March 30, 2017. https://www.washingtonpost.com/news/the-fix/wp/2016/12/19/the-tumultuous-recent-history-of-north-carolinas-bathroom-bill-which-could-be-repealed/.

[203] "Public Facilities Privacy & Security Act." *Wikipedia*, January 29, 2023. https://en.wikipedia.org/wiki/Public_Facilities_Privacy_%26_Security_Act.

[204] Not to be left behind, the much smaller ACC, which governs only the Atlantic Coast Conference of college games, announced it would move its own regional football championship out of the state.

[205] Analysis would find the actual cost afterwards was roughly $600m. See: https://www.forbes.com/sites/corinnejurney/2016/11/03/north-carolinas-bathroom-bill-flushes-away-nearly-1-billion-in-business-and-governor-mccrorys-re-election-hopes/?sh=6eae96df682a

[206] Julie Pace and Jill Colvin, "Attorney General Lynch Tells Transgender Community 'We See You,'" PBS NewsHour, May 10, 2016. https://www.pbs.org/newshour/nation/attorney-general-lynch-tells-transgender-community-we-see-you.

[207] Amber Phillips, "How Loretta Lynch's Speech Brought Some Transgender Advocates to Tears." *Washington Post*, May 11, 2016. https://www.washingtonpost.com/news/the-fix/wp/2016/05/11/loretta-lynchs-speech-just-made-her-a-hero-to-transgender-activists/.

[208] Sheryl Gay Stolberg, "President Obama's Views on Gay Marriage 'Evolving.'" *The New York Times*, February 6, 2013. https://www.nytimes.com/2011/06/19/us/politics/19marriage.html.

[209] "U.S. Departments of Justice and Education Release Joint Guidance To," May 16, 2016. https://www.justice.gov/opa/pr/us-departments-justice-and-education-release-joint-guidance-help-schools-ensure-civil-rights.

[210] David Montgomery and Alan Blinder, "States Sue Obama Administration Over Transgender Bathroom Policy." *The New York Times*, May 26, 2016. https://www.nytimes.com/2016/05/26/us/states-texas-sue-obama-administration-over-transgender-bathroom-policy.html.

[211] https://www.washingtonpost.com/local/education/another-10-states-sue-obama-administration-over-bathroom-guidance-for-transgender-students/2016/07/08/a930238e-4533-11e6-88d0-6adee48be8bc_story.html

[212] In Maine, the governor would be the party suing, and in Arizona and Texas, schools districts would sue.

[213] David Montgomery and Alan Blinder, "States Sue Obama Administration Over Transgender Bathroom Policy." *The New York Times*, May 26, 2016. https://www.nytimes.com/2016/05/26/us/states-texas-sue-obama-administration-over-transgender-bathroom-policy.html.

[214] Emanuella Grinberg, "Feds Issue Guidance on Transgender Access to School Bathrooms." *CNN*, May 14, 2016. https://www.cnn.com/2016/05/12/politics/transgender-bathrooms-obama-administration/index.html.

[215] McCrory also signs a particularly nasty a bill quickly pushed through the legislature that significantly curtails the gubernatorial power Cooper will have.

[216] American Civil Liberties Union. "Supreme Court Allows Gavin Grimm's Victory to Stand | American Civil Liberties Union," June 28, 2021. https://www.aclu.org/press-releases/supreme-court-allows-gavin-grimms-victory-stand.

[217] *Ibid* American Civil Liberties Union. "Supreme Court Allows Gavin Grimm's Victory to Stand | American Civil Liberties Union," June 28, 2021. https://www.aclu.org/press-releases/supreme-court-allows-gavin-grimms-victory-stand.

[218] Nina Totenberg, "Supreme Court Won't Enforce West Virginia Law Banning Trans Athletes from Girls' Teams." *NPR*, April 6, 2023. https://www.npr.org/2023/04/06/1165133771/trans-law-west-virginia-supreme-court.

[219] Hannah Natanson, "Virginia School Board Will Pay $1.3 Million in Settlement to Transgender Student Gavin Grimm, Who Sued over Bathroom Policy." *Washington Post*, August 26, 2021. https://www.washingtonpost.com/local/education/transgender-bathroom-settlement-gavin-grimm/2021/08/26/0f186784-0699-11ec-a266-7c7fe02fa374_story.html.

[220] Jeremy W. Peters, "A Conservative Push to Make Trans Kids and School Sports the Next Battleground in the Culture War." *The New York Times*, August 18, 2020. https://www.nytimes.com/2019/11/03/us/politics/kentucky-transgender-school-sports.html.

[221] "Public Facilities Privacy & Security Act." *Wikipedia*, January 29, 2023. https://en.wikipedia.org/wiki/Public_Facilities_Privacy_%26_Security_Act.

[222] "Bathroom Bill." *Wikipedia*, March 30, 2023. https://en.wikipedia.org/wiki/Bathroom_bill.

[223] Kristina Marusic, "Before You Continue to YouTube," n.d. https://www.logotv.com/news/gjmmz9/texas-lt-gov-dan-patrick-press-conference-privacy-protection-act-senate-bill-6-anti-trans-bathroom-bill.

[224] Lawrence Wright, "America's Future Is Texas." *The New Yorker*, July 3, 2017. https://www.newyorker.com/magazine/2017/07/10/americas-future-is-texas.

[225] Human Rights Campaign, December 6, 2016. https://www.hrc. org/press-releases/new-polling-details-watershed-moment-for-lgbtq-equality-hb2-led-to-pat-mccr.

[226] Jennifer Agiesta, "Poll: 6-in-10 Oppose Bills like the North Carolina Transgender Bathroom Law." *CNN*, May 9, 2016. https://www.cnn.com/2016/05/09/politics/poll-transgender-bathroom-law-north-carolina/.

[227] Gary D. Robertson, "Decade since NC Governor Win, McCrory Trounced in Senate Bid." *AP NEWS*, May 26, 2022. https://apnews.com/article/2022-midterm-elections-pat-mccrory-donald-trump-congress-north-carolina-fbd15a0282fa6d04f22f2dc45cc3e4c0.

[228] Gary D. Robertson, (2022, May 26). Decade since NC governor win, McCrory trounced in Senate bid. *AP NEWS*. https://apnews.com/article/2022-midterm-elections-pat-mccrory-donald-trump-congress-north-carolina-fbd15a0282fa6d04f22f2dc45cc3e4c0

[229] https://www.weekendreading.net/p/hiding-in-plain-sight-the-sources

[230] "Yellow Dog Democrat." *Wikipedia*, October 8, 2022. https://en.wikipedia.org/wiki/Yellow_dog_Democrat.

[231] John Fea, Laura Gifford, R. Marie Griffith, and Lerone A. Martin, "Evangelicalism and Politics," The American Historian, n.d. https://www.oah.org/tah/issues/2018/november/evangelicalism-and-politics/.

[232] Michael Podhorzer, "Congressional 'Class Inversion' or Sectional Reversion?" *Weekend Reading*, April 16, 2023. https://michaelpodhorzer.substack.com/p/congressional-class-inversion-or.

[233] The last, in 2017, was the first, and arguably Trump's sole major legislative achievement.

[234] The CEO of PPRI, Robert P. Jones, is the author of the book *White Too Long,* mentioned above.

[235] "Most Americans Support Pro-LGBTQ Policies, But Are More Divided Over Transgender Sports and Bathroom Policies." *PRRI (Public Religion Research Institute)*, September 2021. https://www.prri.org/wp-content/uploads/2021/09/PRRI-Sep-2021-LGBTQ.pdf.

[236] Daniel Greenberg, Maxine Najle, Ph.D., Natalie Jackson, Ph.D., Oyindamola Bola, Robert P. Jones, Ph.D., "America's Growing Support for Transgender Rights," PPRI, October 16, 2020. https://www.prri.org/research/americas-growing-support-for-transgender-rights/.

[237] Interesting, a 2023 CNN poll would find that 79% of Republicans as whole thought the country had "gone too far" in accepting transgender people—much higher numbers that PRRI was getting.

[238] Michael Lipka and Patricia Tevington, "Attitudes about Transgender Issues Vary Widely among Christians, Religious 'Nones' in U.S." *Pew Research Center*, July 7, 2022. https://www.pewresearch.org/fact-tank/2022/07/07/attitudes-about-transgender-issues-vary-widely-among-christians-religious-nones-in-u-s/.

[239] https://www.washingtonpost.com/politics/2022/11/08/transgender-republican-evangelical-bathrooms/

[240] This is true even in response to huge, world-changing events By way of comparison, when Russia launched an unprovoked land-war against Ukraine, U.S. opinion against Russia only shifted from 41% to 70%. See: https://www.pewresearch.org/short-reads/2023/02/23/what-public-opinion-surveys-found-in-the-first-year-of-the-war-in-ukraine/ ft_2023-02-23_ukraine-roundup_02/ Not that these are comparable issues, but a doubling of public opinion is a rarity even in response to world-changing major events that involve the deaths of tens of thousands of soldiers and innocent civilians.

[241] This compares to just 26% for most other Christian denominations.

[242] Michael Lipka and Patricia Tevington, "Attitudes about Transgender Issues Vary Widely among Christians, Religious 'Nones' in U.S." *Pew Research Center*, July 7, 2022. https://www.pewresearch.org/fact-tank/2022/07/07/attitudes-about-transgender-issues-vary-widely-among-christians-religious-nones-in-u-s/.

[243] On a related note, in 2022 Pew poll found that at least some right to abortion was supported by 60% of white Protestants, 66% of Black Protestants, and even 56% of Catholics. But

that finding reversed among white evangelical Christians, 74% of whom were against any right to abortion, and 86% of whom believed that a fetus is a person. This was more than any other religious group. See: Yonat Shimron, "Survey: White Evangelicals Oppose Abortion; All Other Religious Groups Support It." Religion News Service, May 9, 2022. https://religionnews.com/2022/05/06/survey-white-evangelicals-oppose-abortion-other-religious-groups-support-it/.

[244] Audrey Barrick, "Poll: What Evangelical Leaders Believe about the End Times." *The Christian Post*, March 9, 2011. https://www.christianpost.com/news/poll-what-evangelical-leaders-believe-about-the-end-times.html.

[245] Bgea. "What Is the Rapture? See What the Bible Says." Billy Graham Evangelistic Association, December 28, 2022. https://billygraham.org/answer/what-is-the-rapture/.

[246] Ronald Brownstein, "Trump's Fate in 2024 May Rest on Whether He Can Repeat His Biggest Surprise from 2016." *CNN*, February 14, 2023. https://www.cnn.com/2023/02/14/politics/gop-voters-evangelicals-trump-2024-fault-lines/index.html.

[247] Andrew L. Whitehead and Samuel L. Perry. "Is Christian Nationalism Growing or Declining? Both." *Washington Post*, October 25, 2022. https://www.washingtonpost.com/politics/2022/10/25/republicans-christian-nationalism-midterms/.

[248] The few independents caught in the middle either can't vote in Republican state primaries or—in the handful of states where they can—don't exactly flood the voting booths over attacks on transgender kids.

[249] Thomas B. Edsall, "Opinion | The Republican Strategists Who Have Carefully Planned All of This." *The New York Times*, April 12, 2023. https://www.nytimes.com/2023/04/12/opinion/republican-party-intrusive-government.html.

[250] https://www.prri.org/spotlight/texas-government-anti-transgender-actions-and-texan-views-on-transgender-communities/

[251] Bryce Shreve and Chris Hughes. "Poll: Majority of Kentuckians Oppose Proposed Law on Gender-Affirming

Health Care." *Spectrum News Kentucky*, February 23, 2023.
https://spectrumnews1.com/ky/louisville/news/2023/02/23/ke
ntucky-legislature-transgender-health-care.
[252] Devan Cole, "Kentucky's Democratic Governor Vetoes Anti-
Trans Sports Ban." *CNN*, April 7, 2022. A doubling of *any*
public opinion over just six years is very unusual, even in
response to huge, world-changing events
[253] Eli Yokley. "Kentucky's Beshear Ranks as America's Most
Popular Democratic Governor Ahead of Re-Election Bid."
Morning Consult, January 13, 2023. https://morningconsult.
com/2023/01/12/kentucky-beshear-ranks-as-most-popular-
democratic-governor/.
[254] Zach Montellaro. "Is a Democrat Really the Favorite in the
Kentucky Governor Race?," March 8, 2023. https://www.
politico.com/news/2023/03/08/democrat-kentucky-
govnernor-race-00085917.
[255] Kaanita Iyer and Paradise Afshar. "Kentucky Governor Vetoes
Ban on Gender-Affirming Care for Youth." *CNN*, March 25,
2023. https://www.cnn.com/2023/03/24/politics/kentucky-
veto-gender-affirming-youth-care/index.html.
[256] William Wan, "Kentucky Lawmakers Pass Major Anti-Trans
Law, Overriding Governor's Veto." *Washington Post*, March
29, 2023. https://www.washingtonpost.com/dc-md-va/2023
/03/29/kentucky-anti-transgender-law-override-vote/.
[257] Erin Reed, "Mics Off, 6 Minutes Notice - Anti-Trans
Kentucky Forced Detransition Bill Passes After Shameful
Secr - Democratic Underground," n.d. https://www.demo
craticunderground.com/100217733068.
[258] https://www.dailydot.com/debug/genspect/
[259] In addition, since gay rights has avoided any discussion of the
right gender among gay men or lesbian women, when
Christian fundamentalists base their pitch against affirming
care on "protecting children" it is easy for them to leapfrog to
"protecting children from perverse and obscene adult drag
shows." [259] Cross-gender dressing has always been
particularly disliked by the right and a common means of
harassing and criminalizing LGBTQ+ people, ever since
Columbus, Ohio passed one of the nation's first anti-

crossdressing laws in 1848. Even as late as 2011, wearing opposite sex clothes was still illegal in New York City.

[260] https://en.wikipedia.org/wiki/Unite_the_Right_rally#Introduction

[261] WikiLeaks published his emails in November 2016.

[262] TransExclusionary Radical Feminists or TERF is a name adopted by feminists committed to biological determinism and thus excluding trans women from women's spaces and activities. While they originated the name, it was picked up and wielded by transactivists, whereupon many TERFs began decrying it as a slur and renamed themselves Gender Critical Feminists.

[263] Peter Montgomery, "Values Voter Summit Panelist: 'Divide & Conquer' To Defeat 'Totalitarian' Trans Inclusion Policies." *Right Wing Watch*, October 19, 2017. https://www.rightwing watch.org/post/values-voter-summit-panelist-divide-conquer-to-defeat-totalitarian-trans-inclusion-policies/.

[264] Hélène Barthélemy, "Christian Right Tips to Fight Transgender Rights: Separate the T From," Southern Poverty Law Center, October 23, 2017. https://www.splcenter.org/hatewatch/2017/10/23/christian-right-tips-fight-transgender-rights-separate-t-lgb.

[265] "It's Strategy People!," Parents With Inconvenient Truths About Trans (PITT), February 1, 2022. https://pitt.substack.com/p/its-strategy-people.

[266] Jacob Asmussen, "American Principles Project: Texas' New Pro-Family Fighters." *Texas Scorecard*, November 10, 2021. https://texasscorecard.com/state/american-principles-project-texas-new-pro-family-fighters/.

[267] Jeremy W. Peters, "A Conservative Push to Make Trans Kids and School Sports the Next Battleground in the Culture War." *The New York Times*, August 18, 2020. https://www.nytimes.com/2019/11/03/us/politics/kentucky-transgender-school-sports.html?

[268] The Times editorial and science coverage of trans kids, particularly GAC, have often been horrendous and very unfair. For a detailed analysis, see Tom Scocca's piece in Popula: https://popula.com/2023/01/29/the-worst-thing-we-read-this-week-why-is-the-new-york-times-so-obsessed-with-trans-kids/. However, the Times basic news coverage

has been extremely useful and so I've continued to use it whatever the obviously shortcomings in other areas. However, anything one reads outside of its "hard news" sections should be taken with a grain of skepticism.

[269] The non-problem of trans kids competing in sports matching their gender identity actually inverted a real problem: just two years earlier in February 2017, 17-year-old transgender teen Mack Beggs capped a run of 52 wins and took the Texas State Girls' Wrestling Championship in the 110-pound class. This really *was* a case of a boy competing and winning at girls' sports, and it, predictably, drew intense national attention and an outpouring of hatred for Beggs, who only wrestled in the girls' class because Texas state law forced him to do so. Beggs told ESPN, "I'm like, 'You know what? *Boo* all you want, because you're just hating. You hating ain't going to get me and you nowhere, and I'm just going to keep on doing what I've got to do.'" He added that he was trying to minimize his testosterone, so as not to "cheat," explaining that actually he would rather "wrestle boys, because I'm a guy. It just makes more sense." Despite such defiant public comments, four years later Beggs would confide to *Yahoo! News* that he had undergone intense mental health struggles after graduating high school: "I was in a very dark place. I had to seek out help...." See: Eve Hartley, "Yahoo Is Part of the Yahoo Family of Brands," n.d. https://news.yahoo.com/mack-beggs-transgender-wrestler-who-rose-to-prominence-for-competing-against-women-it-took-a-toll-on-me-191642125.html.

[270] https://www.penncapital-star.com/civil-rights-social-justice/wave-of-transgender-health-care-bans-has-roots-in-past-debates/

[271] Morgan Trau, "Six Transgender Girls Play Sports in Ohio, but GOP Wants Them Out." *Ohio Capital Journal*, February 20, 2023. https://ohiocapitaljournal.com/2023/02/20/six-trans gender-girls-play-sports-in-ohio-but-gop-wants-them-out/.

[272] Kiara Alfonseca, "Anti-Trans Sports Ban Fails in Ohio Legislature." *ABC News*, December 15, 2022. https://abcnews.go.com/US/anti-trans-sports-ban-fails-ohio-legislature/story?id=95151486.

[273] Morgan Trau, "GOP Passes Bill Aiming to Root out 'Suspected' Transgender Female Athletes with Genital Inspection." *Ohio Capital Journal*, June 3, 2022. https://ohiocapitaljournal.com/2022/06/03/gop-passes-bill-aiming-to-root-out-suspected-transgender-female-athletes-with-genital-inspection/.

[274] Will Hobson, "The Fight for the Future of Transgender Athletes." *Washington Post*, April 15, 2021. https://www.washingtonpost.com/sports/2021/04/15/transgender-athletes-womens-sports-title-ix/.

[275] Will Hobson, "The Fight for the Future of Transgender Athletes." *Washington Post*, April 15, 2021. https://www.washingtonpost.com/sports/2021/04/15/transgender-athletes-womens-sports-title-ix/.

[276] David Crary, "Lawmakers Can't Cite Local Examples of Trans Girls in Sports." *AP NEWS*, March 3, 2021. https://apnews.com/article/lawmakers-unable-to-cite-local-trans-girls-sports-914a982545e943ecc1e265e8c41042e7.

[277] https://sadbrowngirl.substack.com/p/transgender-compromise

[278] ESPN.com. "Complaint Targets Transgender HS Track Athletes," June 20, 2019. https://www.espn.com.au/high-school/story/_/id/27015115/complaint-targets-transgender-hs-track-athletes.

[279] Katie Barnes, "The Battle over Title IX and Who Gets to Be a Woman in Sports -- inside the Raging National Debate." *ESPN.Com*, June 23, 2020. https://www.espn.com/espnw/story/_/id/29347507/the-battle-title-ix-gets-woman-sports-raging-national-debate.

[280] "Soule v. Connecticut Association of Schools." Alliance Defending Freedom, April 14, 2023. https://adflegal.org/case/soule-v-connecticut-association-schools.

[281] Karleigh Webb, "Chelsea Mitchell Wins Second Title in Two Weeks at CIAC Open." *Outsports*, February 25, 2020. https://www.outsports.com/2020/2/25/21151031/transgender-chelsea-mitchell-terry-miller-adf-lawsuit-connecticut-track-and-field.

[282] DeVos's extremist family has allegedly funded everything from the launching the Family Research Council, to Trump's efforts to overturn Biden's election.

[283] It is the Conference whose rules enabled Miller and Yearwood to compete as girls.

[284] Will Hobson, "The Fight for the Future of Transgender Athletes." *Washington Post*, April 15, 2021. https://www.washingtonpost.com/sports/2021/04/15/transgender-athletes-womens-sports-title-ix/.

[285] Bianca Quilantan, "2nd Circuit Tosses Connecticut Transgender Athlete Challenge," December 16, 2022. https://www.politico.com/news/2022/12/16/connecticut-transgender-athlete-00074355.

[286] "Barbara Ehardt." *Wikipedia*, March 25, 2023. https://en.wikipedia.org/wiki/Barbara_Ehardt.

[287] "The 2020 Census of American Religion - PRRI," June 2, 2022. https://www.prri.org/research/2020-census-of-american-religion/#page-section-1.

[288] Rebecca Boone, "Idaho Transgender Athlete Ban Is Template for Other States." *AP NEWS*, March 3, 2021. https://apnews.com/article/idaho-falls-idaho-laws-1db9278e3349c21d2951ffc9147f98f0.

[289] Idaho's population is about 1,900,000; about 13% of the U.S. population are teens, and about half of those are boys.

[290] James Dawson, "Idaho House Republicans Unanimously Back Sex Ed Opt-In Bill." *Boise State Public Radio*, March 5, 2021. https://www.boisestatepublicradio.org/politics-government/2021-03-05/idaho-house-republicans-unanimously-back-sex-ed-opt-in-bill.

[291] Cynthia Sewell, "House Committee OKs Bill That Would End Marriage for Anyone under 16 in Idaho." *East Idaho News*, February 26, 2020. https://www.eastidahonews.com/2020/02/house-committee-oks-bill-that-would-end-marriage-for-anyone-under-16-in-idaho/.

[292] Fraidy Reiss, "Child Marriage in the United States: Prevalence and Implications." *Journal of Adolescent Health*, n.d. https://www.jahonline.org/article/S1054-139X(21)00341-4/fulltext.

[293] After enormous political criticism, Ehardt and a colleague would eventually introduce their own, parents-only bill.

[294] Clark Corbin, "Idaho Legislators Push for Discussions about Moving the State's Border with Oregon." *Idaho Capital Sun*,

February 1, 2023. https://idahocapitalsun.com/2023/02/01/
idaho-legislators-push-for-discussions-about-moving-the-
states-border-with-oregon/.

295 The Greater Idaho Movement. "Why Greater Idaho Is the
Right Choice for Wallowa County - the Greater Idaho
Movement," n.d. https://www.greateridaho.org/vote/.

296 Debbie Bryce, "Center Recognizes Nine Hate Groups in
Idaho." Idaho State Journal, June 5, 2015. https://www.
idahostatejournal.com/members/center-recognizes-nine-hate-
groups-in-idaho/article_2fc18774-ec87-11e3-a505-
001a4bcf887a.html.

297 Aryan Nation, America's Promise Ministries, the Neo-Nazi
NSM, Campaign for Radical Truth in History, International
Conspiratological Association, Crew 38 and the Northwest
Hammerskins, Family Home Northwest, Free Edgage Steele

298 Knute Berger, "Greater Idaho and the Ugly History of
Northwest Secession Movements." *Crosscut*, April 15, 2020.
https://crosscut.com/2020/04/greater-idaho-and-ugly-history-
northwest-secession-movements.

299 This dream originated in 2011 with a 4000-word online treatise
by James Wesley, Rawles [*comma his*], in which he called on
survivalists and "preppers" nationwide to come and create a
white Christian nationalist stronghold to survive the coming
liberal social apocalypse. See: Jack Jenkins, "How Big Christian
Nationalism Has Come Courting in North Idaho." Religion
News Service, February 23, 2023. https://religionnews.com
/2023/02/22/how-big-christian-nationalism-has-come-courting-
in-north-idaho/ and James Wesley Rawles, "The American
Redoubt — Move to the Mountain States." SurvivalBlog.com,
n.d. https://survivalblog.com/ redoubt/.

300 "The United States Law Week," n.d. https://news.bloomberg
law. com/us-law-week/transgender-athlete-fight-to-heat-up-
as-legislatures-returns.

301 Of course weirdly, if she gets dunked-on by 6" 4' Brittney
Griner she has no course of action, because that kind of vast
"unfairness" wouldn't count because Brittney isn't trans.

302 https://legislature.idaho.gov/wp-content/uploads/sessioninfo/
2020/legislation/H0500.pdf

[303] "Section 33-6203 – Idaho State Legislature," n.d. https://legislature.idaho.gov/statutesrules/idstat/Title33/T33CH62/SECT33-6203/.

[304] Trudy Ring, "Martina Navratilova Supports Idaho's Ban on Trans Female Athletes." *Advocate.Com*, August 3, 2020. https://www.advocate.com/transgender/2020/8/03/martina-navratilova-supports-idahos-ban-trans-female-athletes.

[305] Martina Navratilova, "The Rules on Trans Athletes Reward Cheats and Punish the Innocent." *The Times*, February 16, 2019. https://www.thetimes.co.uk/article/the-rules-on-trans-athletes-reward-cheats-and-punish-the-innocent-klsrq6h3x?wgu=270525%3Cem%3E54264%3C/em%3E15620701381564%3Cem%3E321a7e4e48&wgexpiry=1569846138&utm%3C/em%3Esource=planit&utm%3Cem%3Emedium=affiliate&utm%3C/em%3Econtent=22278.

[306] Frances Perraudin, "Martina Navratilova Criticised over 'Cheating' Trans Women Comments." *The Guardian*, February 17, 2019. https://www.theguardian.com/sport/2019/feb/17/martina-navratilova-criticised-over-cheating-trans-women-comments.

[307] While endlessly recycled by anti-trans bigots, there is no known record of this happening in the history of organized sports, except for Dora/Heinrich Ratjen who medaled in the high-jump in the 1936 Olympics for Germany under the Nazi's. He was beaten by three women. Apparently born intersex, Dora eventually came to realize their true gender identity was male but they were raised as, and lived as, a girl and then young woman. Later as an adult their official sex designation would change to *male* and they would change their name to "Heinrich." See: https://en.wikipedia.org/wiki/Heinrich_Ratjen

[308] William Lee Adams, "'Insane & Cheating': Navratilova Reignites Criticism over Transgender Women in Sports." *RT International*, February 17, 2019. https://www.rt.com/sport/451682-insane-cheating-navratilova-reignites-criticism-transgender-women-sport/

[309] Josh Berger, "Martina Navratilova Mobbed For Denouncing University Of Pennsylvania's Decision To Nominate Lia Thomas For NCAA's 'Woman Of The Year' Award -

Bounding Into Sports." Bounding Into Sports, July 19, 2022. https://www.boundingintosports.com/2022/07/martina-navratilova-mobbed-for-denouncing-university-of-pennsylvanias-decision-to-nominate-lia-thomas-for-ncaas-woman-of-the-year-award/.

[310] Her transphobic statements would go on to cited in other states' to justify anti-sports bills as well.

[311] Southern Poverty Law Center. "Family Research Council," n.d. https://www.splcenter.org/fighting-hate/extremist-files/group/family-research-council.

[312] "Before You Continue to YouTube," n.d. https://www.logotv.com/news/r5h7ca/martina-navratilova-transphobic-op-ed-cited-conservative-lawmakers

[313] https://en.wikipedia.org/wiki/Robert_H._Knight

[314] Katie Barnes, "The Battle over Title IX and Who Gets to Be a Woman in Sports -- inside the Raging National Debate." *ESPN.Com*, June 23, 2020. https://www.espn.com/espnw/story/_/id/29347507/the-battle-title-ix-gets-woman-sports-raging-national-debate.

[315] Two cisgender women would file in the lawsuit to be heard as well, claiming they had both raced against a transgender athlete at Idaho State University and lost to her.
Andrew Gatti and Michael Carroll, "Transgender Athletes and Sport Participation – Updates in the Hecox v. Little Case | Sports Litigation Alert," n.d. https://sportslitigationalert.com/transgender-athletes-and-sport-participation-updates-in-the-hecox-v-little-case/.

[316] Trudy Ring, "How Runner Lindsay Hecox Is Fighting for Trans Athletes." *Advocate.Com*, August 3, 2021. https://www.advocate.com/exclusives/2021/8/03/how-runner-lindsay-hecox-fighting-trans-athletes.

[317] Madeline Holcombe and Andy Rose, "Federal Judge Says Idaho Cannot Ban Transgender Athletes from Women's Sports Teams." *CNN*, August 18, 2020. https://www.cnn.com/2020/08/18/us/idaho-transgender-athletes-ban-blocked/index.html.

[318] So far the hearings have not been encouraging, with one judge declaring with unique legal insight that there the law couldn't be discriminatory because transgender girls "can play on the

boys' team whether they're transgender or not." See: Jo Yurcaba, "U.S. Appeals Court Considers Idaho Transgender Athletes Ban," May 4, 2021. https://www.nbcnews.com/feature/nbc-out/u-s-appeals-court-considers-idaho-transgender-athletes-ban-n1266245.

319 Jeremy W. Peters, "Why Transgender Girls Are Suddenly the G.O.P.'s Culture-War Focus." *The New York Times*, May 3, 2021. https://www.nytimes.com/2021/03/29/us/politics/transgender-girls-sports.html.

320 Jeremy W. Peters, "Why Transgender Girls Are Suddenly the G.O.P.'s Culture-War Focus." *The New York Times*, May 3, 2021. https://www.nytimes.com/2021/03/29/us/politics/transgender-girls-sports.html.

321 Jeremy W. Peters, "Why Transgender Girls Are Suddenly the G.O.P.'s Culture-War Focus." *The New York Times*, May 3, 2021. https://www.nytimes.com/2021/03/29/us/politics/transgender-girls-sports.html.

322 Youth Statistics - Adolescence - ACT for Youth. "U.S. Teen Demographics," n.d. https://actforyouth.net/adolescence/demographics/.

323 Ryan Chatelain, "Study Estimates Trans Youth Population Has Doubled in 5 Years." *Spectrum News NY1*, June 10, 2022. https://www.ny1.com/nyc/all-boroughs/news/2022/06/10/study-estimates-transgender-youth-population-has-doubled-in-5-years.

324 The Williams Institute estimates there are about 700,000 transyouth aged 13-17 nationwide, and .027% of the US population lives in South Dakota.

325 The Williams Institute at UCLA School of Law. "How Many Adults and Youth Identify as Transgender in the United States? - Williams Institute." Williams Institute, September 27, 2022. https://williamsinstitute.law.ucla.edu/publications/trans-adults-united-states/.

326 Sara Murray, "Republicans build momentum as they drive anti-LGBTQ legislation nationwide." CNN Politics, April 22, 2022. https://www.cnn.com/2022/04/22/politics/republicans-anti-lgbtq-legislation/index.html

327 Eduardo Medina, "Utah Legislature Overrides Governor's Veto of Transgender Athlete Bill." *The New York Times*,

March 25, 2022. https://www.nytimes.com/2022/03/25/us/utah-transgender-athlete-ban-override.html.

[328] https://time.com/6176799/trans-sports-bans-conservative-movement/

[329] Jeremy W. Peters, "Why Transgender Girls Are Suddenly the G.O.P.'s Culture-War Focus." *The New York Times*, May 3, 2021. https://www.nytimes.com/2021/03/29/us/politics/transgender-girls-sports.html.

[330] Sarah Mervosh, Remy Tumin, and Ava Sasani. "Biden Plan Sets New Rules for Transgender Athletes and School Sports." *The New York Times*, April 7, 2023. https://www.nytimes.com/2023/04/06/us/transgender-athletes-title-ix-biden-adminstration.html.

[331] See: https://www.idahostatesman.com/sports/college/mountain-west/boise-state-university/boise-state-basketball/article 243427506.html

[332] Justin McCarthy, "Mixed Views Among Americans on Transgender Issues." *Gallup.Com*, November 20, 2021. https://news.gallup.com/poll/350174/mixed-views-among-americans-transgender-issues.aspx.

[333] Melissa Block, "Americans Are Deeply Divided on Transgender Rights, a Poll Shows." *NPR*, June 29, 2022. https://www.npr.org/2022/06/29/1107484965/transgender-athletes-trans-rights-gender-transition-poll.

[334] Tara Bahrampour, Scott Clement, and Emily Guskin. "Most Americans Oppose Trans Athletes in Female Sports, Poll Finds." *Washington Post*, June 14, 2022. https://www.washingtonpost.com/dc-md-va/2022/06/13/washington-post-umd-poll-most-americans-oppose-transgender-athletes-female-sports/

[335] The Post found slightly more support for transgirls' playing sports in younger grades, and slightly less support for their playing in college and professional sports.

[336] https://thehill.com/opinion/campaign/4176934-three-states-polls-show-why-republicans-are-all-in-on-transgender-legislation/

[337] Anne Branigin and N. Kirkpatrick, "Anti-Trans Laws Are on the Rise. Here's a Look at Where — and What Kind." *Washington Post*, October 14, 2022. https://www.washingtonpost.com/lifestyle/2022/10/14/anti-trans-bills/.

---

338 A 2023 Washington Post/ KFF found that two-thirds of trans people (66%) know before they're adults that they're trans, including a third (32%) who know when they're still children. Casey Parks, Emily Guskin, and Scott Clement, "Most Trans Adults Say Transitioning Made Them More Satisfied with Their Lives." *Washington Post*, March 23, 2023. https://www.washingtonpost.com/dc-md-va/2023/03/23/transgender-adults-transitioning-poll/.

339 Even so-called transgender "parental notification" laws, which require schools to out a transgender child to their parents—even if the parents were totally opposed and abusing them at home for gender non-conforming behavior (perhaps *especially* so)—is run from the same, anti-gay 1980s playbook, when parents who were religiously opposed to homosexuality demanded that schools had a legal duty to inform them if they suspected that their child might be gay so that it could be "treated."

340 https://www.youtube.com/watch?v=bnP_WoeNuwA

341 https://read.dukeupress.edu/tsq/article/9/3/407/319361/Insidious-ConcernTrans-Panic-and-the-Limits-of

342 https://www.heritage.org/gender/commentary/protect-good-medicine-stop-the-censorship-good-counseling

343 https://www.glaad.org/gap/ryan-t-anderson

344 This was by the nonpartisan GuideStar which compiles information on foundations, and nonprofits.

345 Sumanas W. Jordan and Julia Corcoran, "Considerations in Breast Augmentation in the Adolescent Patient." *Seminars in Plastic Surgery*, February 13, 2013. https://doi.org/10.1055/s-0033-1343998.

346 Ryan Adamczeski, "More Teens Get Breast Implants Than Trans Top Surgery." *Advocate.Com*, September 28, 2022. https://www.advocate.com/transgender/2022/9/28/more-teens-get-breast-implants-trans-top-surgery.

347 Lori Ann Fowler, "Breast Implants for Graduation? Parent and Adolescent Narratives - ProQuest," n.d. https://www.proquest.com/openview/4c6112e57fc4177a56692f1b8837bf0c/1?pq-origsite=gscholar&cbl=18750.

348 Semin Plast Surg. 2013 Feb; 27(1): 67–71. doi: 10.1055/s-0033-1343998 PMCID: PMC3706052 PMID: 24872743

Considerations in Breast Augmentation in the Adolescent Patient Sumanas W. Jordan, MD, PhD1 and Julia Corcoran, MD, FACS, FAAP2

[349] Tom Scocca, "The worst thing we read this week: Why Is the New York Times So Obsessed With Trans Kids?," January 29, 2023. https://popula.com/2023/01/29/the-worst-thing-we-read-this-week-why-is-the-new-york-times-so-obsessed-with-trans-kids/.

[350] https://www.ncbi.nlm.nih.gov/pmc/articles/PMC3706052/

[351] Kari Paul, "More than 200,000 Teens Had Plastic Surgery Last Year, and Social Media Had a Lot to Do with It." *MarketWatch*, September 30, 2018. https://www.market watch.com/story/should-you-let-your-teenager-get-plastic-surgery-2018-08-29.

[352] John S Fuqua, "Treatment and Outcomes of Precocious Puberty: An Update." *The Journal of Clinical Endocrinology & Metabolism* 98, no. 6 (June 1, 2013). https://doi.org/10.1210/jc.2013-1024.

[353] Michelle Conlin, Robin Respaut, and Chad Terhune, "A Gender Imbalance Emerges among Trans Teens Seeking Treatment," November 18, 2022. https://www.reuters.com/investigates/special-report/usa-transyouth-topsurgery/.

[354] A study published in the Journal of the American Medical Association of all transgender surgeries from found that about 8% or were for those ages 12-18 or 3,678, which works out to about 736 per year. However, that includes 18-year-olds, who are legally adults in terms of personal medical decisions and no longer considered minors. https://www.nytimes.com/2023/08/23/health/transgender-surgery.html?smid=nytcore-android-share

[355] Francesca Paris, "Bans on Transition Care for Young People Spread Across U.S." *The New York Times*, April 17, 2023. https://www.nytimes.com/2023/04/15/upshot/bans-transgender-teenagers.html.

[356] https://jrlatham.com/post/181232045264/trans-men-and-the-meaning-of-man

[357] Rates of IGM have finally begun falling in recent years.

[358] Some intersex activists prefer the term Disorders of Sexual Development, feeling that it is a condition, not (like transgender) an identity.

[359] Jules Gill-Peterson would point out in her Histories of the Transgender Child that it was only Johns Hopkins "experimenting on intersex children's unfinished bodies [that] provided the founding protocols of sex assignment *and* reassignment for all human bodies, including those who would be called transvestites and transsexuals..." [p 77]

[360] Montana Senator Did Not Even Read His Own Anti-trans Bill, Jan 27, 2023, https://www.erininthemorning.com/p/montana-senator-did-not-even-read

[361] This exception would actually be seized on by organizations suing to stop implementation of these measures, since it's against the law to allow the same procedures for one group while outlawing them for another simply because its disfavored.

[362] https://twitter.com/assignedmedia/status/1697267033413496970

[363] This includes those suffering from urological abnormalities, cancer surgeries, men with irreparable impotence, ciswomen born with partial or missing vaginas (i.e., vaginal agenesis), unnecessary cosmetic procedures on intersex infants, and wound survivors—including more recently injuries from IEDs which explode upward and often injure the groin.

[364] Jeffrey M. Jones, "U.S. LGBT Identification Steady at 7.2%." *Gallup.Com*, February 17, 2023. https://news.gallup.com/poll/470708/lgbt-identification-steady.aspx.

[365] This is obviously a pretty wide variation. The problem is, the smaller the fraction of a population being polled, the harder it is to get a precise percentage, because just a few extra "hits" a sample skew the results dramatically.

[366] Susan Miller, "Gen Z Is Driving Force among Adults Identifying as LGBTQ, Poll Shows. Here's a Breakdown." *USA TODAY*, February 23, 2023. https://www.usatoday.com/story/news/nation/2023/02/22/gallup-poll-lgbtq-identification/11309075002/.

[367] Jeffrey M. Jones, "U.S. LGBT Identification Steady at 7.2%." *Gallup.Com*, February 17, 2023. https://news.gallup.com/poll/470708/lgbt-identification-steady.aspx.

[368] While the Williams Institute found someone smaller increases for Gen Z, Pew found their trans identification growing even higher, to 3.1% See: Brown, "About 5% of Young Adults in the U.S. Say Their Gender Is Different from Their Sex Assigned at Birth." *Pew Research Center*, June 7, 2022. https://www.pewresearch.org/fact-tank/2022/06/07/about-5-of-young-adults-in-the-u-s-say-their-gender-is-different-from-their-sex-assigned-at-birth/.

[369] The biggest jump in trans identification is for those identifying "off the binary," as something other than "trans man" or "trans woman," as nonbinary, genderqueer, and so on. Similarly, by far the biggest jump in LGB identification is not gays or lesbians, but among bisexuals.

[370] Total LGBTQ+ identification increased by the following:

Generation Z	1997 to 2004/2012	19.7%
Millennials	1981 to 1996	11.2%
Generation X	1965 to 1980	3.3%
Baby Boomers	1946 to 1964	2.7%

[371] This is considered to include the years 1997 through 2012, but Gallup only polled adults 18 and over, so their cut-off was 2003.

[372] https://www.statnews.com/2022/10/03/gender-affirming-surgery-hospitals-johns-hopkins/

[373] Hopkins would apologize four decades later, and reopen its clinic, although only for evaluations and hormone treatment. https://archive.thinkprogress.org/johns-hopkins-transgender-surgery-5c9c428184c1/

[374] https://en.wikipedia.org/wiki/Paul_R._McHugh#Introduction

[375] Theresa Gaffney, "'History Is Repeating Itself': The Story of the Nation's First Clinic for Gender-Affirming Surgery." *STAT*, October 4, 2022. https://www.statnews.com/2022/10/03/gender-affirming-surgery-hospitals-johns-hopkins/.

[376] By mid-2023 Republicans were already calling for banning *all* gender affirming are for youth *and* adults. Just as sports was just a jumping off point for attack pediatric care, kids were was just a launching pad for banning transgender adults as well. See: https://news.yahoo.com/trans-adults-too-gop-candidates-170053762.html?guccounter=1&guce_referrer=aHR0cHM6Ly90LmNvLw&guce_referrer_sig=AQAAAI4e

VEf1HJpKYU57mNxq0KAYpGpddx0dNlWNQ-
8RdfyGiOvgfSX39uT4s1vIZPSrc5l0r9jRk3mfS96e2R7nhn
VU3sVYU06xPgh9K8-8cRz57LtRPQBUtDQSzS3_A5FR
mKILTd59CT3pUP-Lg2cCbUIOD3KE1rtsl9HKfoInu2qq

[377] When I went looking for information for my own transition in 1978, there was one book: Harry Benjamin's *The Transsexual Phenomenon* (although I didn't feel very phenomenal at the time). In a city of over one million, there were only two other "out" transsexuals. Private doctors were uncomfortable or hostile and knew even less than I did. While I finally found treatment, I promptly lost my partner of seven years, my home, and my job. I was frequently harassed, and at my new job most colleagues literally shunned me.

[378] Using Gallup's lower figure of 1.9% it would be 1.3m; with Pew's 3.1% it would be 2.1m.

[379] https://www.aecf.org/blog/generation-z-statistics

[380] https://explodingtopics.com/blog/gen-z-stats

[381] https://www.pewresearch.org/religion/2021/05/11/the-size-of-the-u-s-jewish-population/

[382] https://wisevoter.com/state-rankings/mormon-population-by-state/#:~:text=Culture-,Introduction,living%20in%20the%20United%20States.

[383] Azeen Ghorayshi, "Report Reveals Sharp Rise in Transgender Young People in the U.S." *The New York Times*, June 10, 2022. https://www.nytimes.com/2022/06/10/science/transgender-teenagers-national-survey.html.

[384] It will eventually do so after several failed attempts in 2023.

[385] The acronym is stands for GENder Education and Care, Interdisciplinary Support program.

[386] Personal communication with author January, 2023.

[387] Personal communication with author January, 2023.

[388] The first is at Texas Children's Hospital and the third Legacy Community Health.

[389] Scott Farwell, "Children's Medical Center Dallas Opens Clinic for Transgender Children and Teenagers," n.d. https://interactives.dallasnews.com/2015/gender/.

[390] Sadly only a few years later, the generally pro-trans Dallas Morning news would call for laws and policies that would

force schools to out trans students to their parents, although this might expose them to abuse.

[391] Judge Kim Cooks The 255™ Judicial District Court Memorandum Ruling Final Trial--—October 15-21, 2019 Itio GEORGULAS V. YOUNGER df-15-09887

[392] Karen Zraick, "Texas Father Says 7-Year-Old Isn't Transgender, Igniting a Politicized Outcry." *The New York Times*, October 28, 2019. https://www.nytimes.com/2019/10/28/us/texas-transgender-child.html.

[393] IBID Judge Kim Cooks The 255™ Judicial District Court Memorandum Ruling Final Trial--—October 15-21, 2019 Itio GEORGULAS V. YOUNGER df-15-09887

[394] IGM of course is an unfortunate exception here.

[395] IBID Judge Kim Cooks The 255™ Judicial District Court Memorandum Ruling Final Trial--—October 15-21, 2019 Itio GEORGULAS V. YOUNGER df-15-09887

[396] Katelyn Burns, "Republican Lawmakers Are in a Rush to Regulate Every Trans Kid's Puberty." *Vox*, January 29, 2020. https://www.vox.com/identities/2020/1/29/21083505/transgender-kids-legislation-puberty-blockers.

[397] Mimi Swartz, "Who Is Greg Abbott?" *Texas Monthly*, November 14, 2022. https://www.texasmonthly.com/news-politics/who-is-greg-abbott/.

[398] Mimi Swartz, "Who Is Greg Abbott?" *Texas Monthly*, November 14, 2022. https://www.texasmonthly.com/news-politics/who-is-greg-abbott/.

[399] Christopher Hooks, "Greg Abbott's Voter Suppression Methods Have Become More Subtle—But They're Still Transparent." *Texas Monthly*, March 15, 2021. https://www.texasmonthly.com/news-politics/abbott-ballot-drop-offs-vote-suppression/.

[400] Mimi Swartz, "Who Is Greg Abbott?" *Texas Monthly*, November 14, 2022. https://www.texasmonthly.com/news-politics/who-is-greg-abbott/.

[401] Katelyn Burns, "Republican Lawmakers Are in a Rush to Regulate Every Trans Kid's Puberty." *Vox*, January 29, 2020. https://www.vox.com/identities/2020/1/29/21083505/transgender-kids-legislation-puberty-blockers.

---

[402] Connecticut was first in May 2022, followed by Massachusetts that July, and finally California the following September. In early 2023, Gov. Tim Walz will issue an E.O. making Minnesota the fourth sanctuary state. California's law is surprisingly comprehensive stating that it will not enforce out-of-state laws, honor subpoenas, reply to requests for information, or participate in arrests or extraditions connected to attacks on pediatric gender care. By mid 2023 the number of states with trans sanctuary laws would mushroom from three to 14, as Arizona, Colorado, Illinois, Maryland, Minnesota, New Jersey, New Mexico, New York, Oregon, Vermont, and Washington also enacted protections. See: https://www.wsj.com/articles/transgender-america-fights-back-a2c841f0?mod=hp_lead_pos8

[403] Although denial of medical care cannot be compared with the horrors of chattel slavery, abortion and affirming care are now recapitulating the geopolitical pattern established by antebellum slavery laws, in which primarily Southern states passed laws demanding the punishment and/or return of enslaved individuals. In response, primarily Northern and Western states passed laws protecting those who sought refuge within their borders. Blue states where similar legislation was introduced in 2022 which have reasonable-to-good chances of passage include Colorado, Illinois, Maine, Michigan, Minnesota, New Hampshire, New Mexico, New York, Oregon, Rhode Island, Vermont, and Washington. Since pro and anti-GAC states are completely at odds over issues of law and jurisdiction, the issue will be eventually decided by the federal courts, as also happened with slavery and abortion.

[404] The others are Montana, North Dakota and Nevada, each of literally which have more livestock than people.

[405] The majority opinion holds that "It is impossible to discriminate against a person for being... transgender without discriminating... based on sex," This argument—that the transgender community should be protected under Title VII of the Civil Rights Act of 1964, which bars employment discrimination based on sex—had been pushed by trans lawyers at least since the 1990s, and it was one the gay legal

community only slowly adopted, often thanks to the quiet work of legal scholar, professor, and gay rights advocate, Chai Feldblum.

[406] https://www.theatlantic.com/politics/archive/2021/01/evangelicals-catholics-jericho-march-capitol/617591/

[407] KARK.com. "Gov. Sarah Huckabee Sanders Signs Seven Executive Orders on First Day in Office," January 10, 2023. https://www.kark.com/news/your-local-election-hq/gov-sarah-huckabee-sanders-signs-seven-executive-orders-on-first-day-in-office/.

[408] "Meet Arkansas State Representative Robin Lundstrum|Lundstrum for Arkansas," n.d. https://lundstrum4arkansas.com/about-robin/.

[409] Arkansas State Legislature. "HB1570 Bill Information," n.d. https://www.arkleg.state.ar.us/Bills/Detail?id=hb1570&ddBienniumSession=2021%2F2021R&Search=.

[410] "Arkansas House Bill 1570 (2021)." *Wikipedia*, February 26, 2023. https://en.wikipedia.org/wiki/Arkansas_House_Bill_1570_(2021)#:~:text=Arkansas%20House%20Bill%201570%20(HB,therapy,%20and%20sex%20reassignment%20surgery.

[411] Personal communication with author, Jan 29, 2023.

[412] https://www.nytimes.com/2021/04/08/us/politics/asa-hutchinson-arkansas-transgender-law.html

[413] Sneha Dey, "Abbott Says He Backs Ban on Transgender Athletes at College Level." *Chron*, February 12, 2023. https://www.chron.com/news/houston-texas/article/abbott-says-backs-ban-transgender-athletes-17780136.php.

[414] Kyle Morris, "Indiana Republican Governor Vetoes Bill barring Transgender Girls from Female Sports." *Fox News*, March 23, 2022. https://www.foxnews.com/politics/indiana-governor-vetoes-transgender-sports-bill.

[415] James Macpherdon, "North Dakota Gov. Burgum Vetoes Transgender Sports Measure." *AP NEWS*, April 22, 2021. https://apnews.com/article/sports-north-dakota-government-and-politics-8ddd363288233d6c0ca85d0ddc75b5c2.

[416] Adam Beam, "Bevin Rules out Bill Restricting Transgender Bathroom Use." *Commonwealth Journal*, December 10, 2016. https://www.somerset-kentucky.com/news/bevin-rules-

out-bill-restricting-transgender-bathroom-use/article_
31f7f82c-be51-11e6-a5a8-e79299967b97.html.

[417] If Cox thought that banning a few transgirls from playing
school sports would increase rates of suicide, it is unclear
how he thought refusing them all medical care and forcing
those already receiving it through a forced detransition would
do *less* harm. Yet just 10 months later, Cox makes make
Utah the first state of 2023 to pass an anti-care bill into law,
joining Alabama, Arkansas, Arizona, and Tennessee. He
justifies it by decrying the "permanent and life-altering
treatments" for a few hundred trans kids, but says nothing
about the thousands of cisgender kids in his state receiving
exactly the same "permanent and life-altering" procedures.
See: Jessica Corbett, "GOP Utah Gov. Signs Ban on
'Lifesaving Medical Care' for Trans Youth." *Common
Dreams*, January 30, 2023. https://www.commondreams.org
/news/utah-transgender-youth-healthcare-cox.

[418] Less than six months later in August 2022, it will turn out
Utah's cisgender girls aren't completely immune from these
laws either. The Utah High School Athletics Association
(UHSA) will report that it has secretly investigated a
cisgender athlete, without informing her or her parents, after
she had won a race "by a wide margin" and the second and
third place finishers file complaints alleging that she must be
transgender. UHSA will dig all the way back through her
middle school, elementary school, and finally kindergarten
records, before determining that she had always been
registered as female and concluding that since it was unlikely
she had transitioned before kindergarten, she was probably
not transgender. It explains that no one was told, to spare the
girl "embarrassment" of being accused of being trans.

[419] Andrew Demillo, "Arkansas Governor Vetoes Transgender
Youth Treatment Ban." *AP NEWS*, April 6, 2021. https://
apnews.com/article/arkansas-legislature-us-news-legislation-
asa-hutchinson-83d07a502678f9745bb00f91 aa4865f6.

[420] Ronald J. Krotoszynski, Jr., "The War on Trans Kids Is
Totally Unconstitutional." *The Atlantic*, May 19, 2021.
https://www.theatlantic.com/ideas/archive/2021/05/anti-
transgender-children-laws-unconstitutional/618864/.

[421] Krotoszynsky would also add that "Since the 1970s, the Supreme Court has consistently rejected moral disapproval of a particular group of individuals as a constitutionally legitimate basis for imposing targeted legal burdens on the group…" This is the same legal principle the Court would rely on it is landmark *Lawrence v. Texas* ruling in 2003, striking down Texas's ban on same-sex intimacy.

[422] Personal communicate with author, Jan 29, 2023

[423] Trudy Ring, "Arkansas Just Made It Easier to Sue Providers of Gender-Affirming Care." *Advocate.Com*, March 15, 2023. https://www.advocate.com/politics/gender-affirming-care-arkansas-sue.

[424] Brendan Pierson, "Arkansas Loses Renewed Bid to Revive Ban on Gender-Affirming Care for Minors." *Reuters*, November 16, 2022. https://www.reuters.com/legal/govern ment/arkansas-loses-renewed-bid-revive-ban-gender-affirming-care-minors-2022-11-16/.

[425] Not to be denied Arkansas, legislators would work closely with Christian evangelical groups to craft a new law allowing anyone receiving affirming care as a child to sue for malpractice lawsuit for up to 15 years after they attain adult-hood, or until age 33. It would make it virtually impossible for the state's care-providing doctors to get malpractice insurance, the kind of extra-legal work-around that would be used in Texas and then Florida. Huckabee Sanders signed the bill into law.

[426] Doni Holloway, "Why Is This Happening? Discussing the Fixation on Anti-Trans Legislation with Chase Strangio," April 5, 2023. https://www.msnbc.com/msnbc-podcast/why-is-this-happening/discussing-fixation-anti-trans-legislation-chase-strangio-podcast-transcript-n1304130.

[427] Ben Rowen. "Don Huffines Won the War of Ideas. Did It Cost Him a Chance to Unseat Greg Abbott?" *Texas Monthly*, February 12, 2022. https://www.texasmonthly.com/news-politics/don-huffines-governor-campaign-greg-abbott/.

[428] Karen Brooks Harper, "Jeff Younger's Custody Battle Sparked Texas' Anti-Transgender-Care Turn." *The Texas Tribune*, March 14, 2022. https://www.texastribune.org/2022/03/14/jeff-younger-transgender-care-house/.

[429] Jacob Asmussen, "American Principles Project Releases New Ad Exhorting Gov. Abbott to Outlaw Child Mutilation Experiments." *Texas Scorecard*, February 14, 2022. https://texasscorecard.com/state/american-principles-project-releases-new-ad-exhorting-gov-abbott-to-outlaw-child-mutilation-experiments/.

[430] Jacob Asmussen, "American Principles Project: Texas' New Pro-Family Fighters." *Texas Scorecard*, November 10, 2021. https://texasscorecard.com/state/american-principles-project-texas-new-pro-family-fighters/.

[431] Jacob Asmussen, "American Principles Project Launches $1M Ad Campaign Exhorting Gov. Abbott to Outlaw Child Mutilation Experiments." *Texas Scorecard*, February 4, 2022. https://texasscorecard.com/state/american-principles-project-launches-1m-ad-campaign-admonishing-gov-abbott-to-outlaw-child-mutilation-experiments/.

[432] Jacob Asmussen, "Gov. Abbott, State Officials Still Won't Act to Ban Child Mutilation in Texas." *Texas Scorecard*, January 12, 2022. https://texasscorecard.com/state/gov-abbott-state-officials-still-wont-act-to-ban-child-mutilation-in-texas/.

[433] Jacob Asmussen, "Texas House Republicans Refuse to Outlaw Child Mutilation Procedures." *Texas Scorecard*, May 18, 2021. https://texasscorecard.com/state/texas-house-republicans-refuse-to-outlaw-child-mutilation-procedures/.

[434] Another similar bill would also fail in May of 2023.See: https://tfn.org/sb-14-fails-to-advance/

[435] In 2023, Paxton will settle with his staff, agreeing to pay four of the eight $3.3m. Not from his own pocket of course, but out of state coffers. The legislature would balk, and Paxton would be impeached by his own Republican-led colleagues, 121-23 See: https://thehill.com/homenews/statewatch/4022975-ag-ken-paxton-impeached-texas-house/

[436] Interestingly, Patton's "bespoke" legal opinion to try to end trans care was not a one-off. Among the key transgressions cited by his Republican colleagues in impeaching him was a tendency to use the A.G.'s office to lawlessly issue such opinions, including one which suddenly blocked foreclosure sales throughout the state issued just in time to save an important donor losing 13 properties at auction.

[437] "Memorandum Ruling." *301st Judicial District Court | Judge Mary Brown*, August 3, 2021. https://thetexan.news/wp-content/uploads/2021/08/df-15-09887_Memorandum_Ruling.pdf.

[438] Although being trans has nothing to do with sexuality, this is evangelical Christian organizations' effort to connect transgender with the *sexualizing of kids* and is the same frame it will adopt in the coming attacks on drag queens.

[439] Jasper Scherer, "Prompted by Abbott Challenger, Texas Agency Removes Webpage with Suicide Hotline for LGBTQ Youths." *Houston Chronicle*, October 13, 2021. https://www.houstonchronicle.com/politics/texas/article/Prompted-by-Abbott-primary-challenger-Texas-16525826.php.

[440] "…born with a medically verifiable genetic disorder of sex development, such as the presence of both ovarian and testicular tissue; or who does not have the normal sex chromosome structure for male or female as determined through genetic testing."

[441] Personal communication with author, Jan 21 2023.

[442] She was eventually able to speak publicly, but only as a private citizen and not in any official capacity.

[443] Azeen Ghorayashi, "Texas Youth Gender Clinic Closed Last Year Under Political Pressure." *The New York Times*, March 8, 2022. https://www.nytimes.com/2022/03/08/health/texas-transgender-clinic-genecis-abbott.html.

[444] Sneha Dey, "Texas Trans Teens Shut out from Medical Care amid GOP Efforts." *The Texas Tribune*, March 23, 2022. https://www.texastribune.org/2022/03/22/texas-transgender-teenagers-medical-care/.

[445] Sneha Dey, "Texas Children's Hospital in Houston Halts Trans Kids' Hormone Therapies." *The Texas Tribune*, March 9, 2022. https://www.texastribune.org/2022/03/04/texas-transgender-children-hormone-therapy/.

[446] Jacob Asmussen, "Gov. Abbott, State Officials Still Won't Act to Ban Child Mutilation in Texas." *Texas Scorecard*, January 12, 2022. https://texasscorecard.com/state/gov-abbott-state-officials-still-wont-act-to-ban-child-mutilation-in-texas/.

[447] Eleanor Klibanoff, "Ken Paxton Investigates Pharmaceutical Companies over Puberty Blockers." *The Texas Tribune*,

March 24, 2023. https://www.texastribune.org/2022/03/ 24/transgender-texas-paxton-pharmaceutical/.

[448] The charge itself is risible: drugs are often prescribed "off-label" once they have been approved by the FDA as safe and effective in one context, because getting re-approval for every subsequent use would be time-intensive and costly— besides not being required by the FDA. Nonetheless many states that go on to ban care will go on to cite this as a key justification: it's basically just a good-sounding lie.

[449] Paisley Currah, "Sex Is as Sex Does: Governing Transgender Identity," 9780814717103: Amazon.Com: Books," n.d. https://www.amazon.com/Sex-Does-Governing-Trans gender-Identity/dp/0814717101.

[450] The assault is not limited solely to affirming medical care: Abbott declares that anyone with knowledge of care who fails to report it also risk civil and/or criminal charges.

[451] A few days earlier, Paxton had finally defeated Krause and his two other challengers in the A.G. primary. He and George P. Bush would face each other in the May 25 runoff election. See: "Ken Paxton And George P. Bush Advance To May Runoff In GOP Texas Attorney General Primary." *CBS News*, March 3, 2022. https://www.cbsnews.com/dfw/news/ ken-paxton-george-p-bush-runoff-gop-texas-attorney-general/.

[452] In Houston alone, DFPS's own data show that CPS seizes Black kids 3.5 times more often than white kids.

[453] By 2023, in another, Paxton would harness state agencies in one more extra-legal attempt to attack trans people, asking them to create a secret database of 16,000 of citizens who had changed the sex on their state identification documents. The purposes of this is never revealed, but the mind reels with the uses to which a hostile Attorney General's office could put it in tracking and surveilling Texas's transgender population. See: Molly Hennessy-Fiske, "Texas Attorney General's Office Sought State Data on Transgender Texans." *Washington Post*, December 14, 2022. https://www.washingtonpost.com/nation/2022/12/14/ texas-transgender-data-paxton/.

[454] According to Pew, white evangelicals are still the only major religious group that believes prioritizing precreation is best for society. See: https://www.pewresearch.org/short-

reads/2021/12/16/white-evangelicals-more-likely-than-other-christians-to-say-people-should-prioritize-marriage-procreation/

455 "Texas Eugenics," n.d. https://www.uvm.edu/~lkaelber/eugenics/TX/TX.html#:~:text=The%20asylums%20were%20meant%20to,27.

456 Alexandra Stern, "Forced Sterilization Policies in the US Targeted Minorities and Those with Disabilities – and Lasted into the 21st Century," Institute for Healthcare Policy & Innovation, n.d. https://ihpi.umich.edu/news/forced-sterilization-policies-us-targeted-minorities-and-those-disabilities-and-lasted-21st#:~:text=Indiana%20passed%20the%20world's%20first,an%20international%20leader%20in%20eugenics.

457 Religion & Politics. "Religion & Politics," n.d. https://religionandpolitics.org/.

458 "Eugenics Archive Theme," n.d. http://www.eugenicsarchive.org/eugenics/topics_fs.pl?theme=8.

459 Caitlin Gibson, "Texas Is Home. The Briggle Family and Their Trans Child Are Fighting for It." *Washington Post*, April 10, 2023. https://www.washingtonpost.com/parenting/2023/04/10/texas-trans-children-families/.

460 Kate Sosin, "Texas AG Ken Paxton Once Joined This Family of a Trans Kid for Dinner. They Now Feel under Attack," PBS NewsHour, February 25, 2022. https://www.pbs.org/newshour/nation/texas-ag-ken-paxton-once-joined-this-family-of-a-trans-kid-for-dinner-they-now-feel-under-attack.

461 Personal communication with author, Dec 2022.

462 While the Briggles' dinner experience with Paxton may be a sign that he's not a true-blue hater, as one local reporter would confide after covering him, "he's still a sack of sh*t."

463 This is an alias as she has asked to remain anonymous for reasons of safety.

464 Lawrence Wright, "America's Future Is Texas." *The New Yorker*, July 3, 2017. https://www.newyorker.com/magazine/2017/07/10/americas-future-is-texas.

465 Casey Parks, "He Came out as Trans. Then Texas Had Him Investigate Parents of Trans Kids." *Washington Post*, September 23, 2022. https://www.washingtonpost.com/dc-

md-va/2022/09/23/texas-transgender-child-abuse-
investigations/.

[466] According to reports, staff would post about this investigation
on an internal CPS listserv. In an agency infamous for a huge
backlog even for the most dire cases, other staff would be
understandably incredulous, all but accusing those doing the
posting of lying. One would reportedly point out that such
investigations couldn't possibly be true, because she has been
waiting months for CPS to investigate an active case of
probable child abuse.

[467] Caitlin Gibson, "Texas Is Home. The Briggle Family and
Their Trans Child Are Fighting for It." *Washington Post*,
April 10, 2023. https://www.washingtonpost.com/parenting
/2023/04/10/texas-trans-children-families/.

[468] Casey Parks, "He Came out as Trans. Then Texas Had Him
Investigate Parents of Trans Kids." *Washington Post*,
September 23, 2022. https://www.washingtonpost.com/dc-
md-va/2022/09/23/texas-transgender-child-abuse-
investigations/.

[469] As supervisor Randa Mulanax, one of the few brave enough to
speak despite certain reprisal, would confirm, "You cannot
Priority-None these cases." On the contrary, all trans cases
are to be classified as Priority-One: *investigate immediately.*
Caseworker Shelby McCowen, who also bravely speaks out,
tell the A/P that trans families are essentially being given the
same priority as child death investigations. See; Paul J.
Weber, "Caseworkers: Texas Order on Trans Kids Handled
Differently." The Detroit News. *Associated Press*, April 1,
2022. https://www.detroitnews.com/story/news/politics/
2022/04/01/caseworkers-texas-order-trans-kids-handled-
differently/7244551001/.

[470] As Davis would recall, "A lot of them are single mothers with
kids, who need the job and insurance. They're vulnerable and
they couldn't afford to leave. They've dedicated their entire
lives to this. You take the crap hours and the crap pay
because you care deeply about children – and they did this
for us. Personal communication with author, Jan 21, 2023.

[471] Davis will be the last person to leave in his five person Travis
County unit. In the coming month, 50% of Travis County

DFPS personnel quit, including 12 of the original 13 supervisors. According to news reports, this pattern is being repeated across DFPS state-wide, as nearly 2,300 of 13,000 employees leave their jobs. It is the highest voluntary exit rate since DFPS became independent in 2017, leading a federal judge to observe that the agency is teetering "on the brink of collapse. All of them are immediately replaced, from the supervisors on down, usually by untrained recruits with no experience in child welfare. See: Andy Rose, "Texas' Family Services Are 'on the Brink of Collapse' after Requiring Child Abuse Investigations of Gender-Affirming Care for Minors, Employees Say in Court Filing." *CNN*, September 1, 2022. https://www.cnn.com/2022/09/01/us/texas-gender-affirming-care-minors-agency-employees-court-filing/index.html.

[472] Katelyn Burns, "The Battle over Luna Younger, a 7-Year-Old Trans Girl in Texas, Explained." *Vox*, November 11, 2019. https://www.vox.com/identities/2019/11/11/20955059/luna-younger-transgender-child-custody.

[473] Altogether, across all the nearly two dozen anti-trans states, Data for Progress surveys found that about 8% of transgender adults have moved to avoid restrictive laws and/or policies. That would amount to about 100-200k. And that doesn't count the families with transgender children who have been forced to leave their states, which might be an additional 100k. Altogether these laws have created a new class of internally displaced political refugees of the sort not seen in the U.S. since perhaps before the Civil War, when enslaved African Americans fled southern states under the terrible regime of chattel slavery. See Data For Progress here: https://www.dataforprogress.org/blog/2023/6/8/lgbtq-adults-do-not-feel-safe-and-do-not-think-the-democratic-party-is-doing-enough-to-protect-their-rights. See also Erin the Morning blog here: https://www.erininthemorning.com/p/us-internal-refugee-crisis-130-260k?utm_source=post-email-title&publication_id=994764&post_id=128030308&isFreemail=false

[474] Other parents fleeing other states were luckier. I was commiserating with one Idaho mother on the wrenching loss of the life she had left behind,. She corrected me: she had lived in the state's long, narrow, northern "chimney" and

"the Washington state line was literally right across the bridge." She'd even been able to keep her original job—which had been over in Washington anyway.

[475] Caitlin Gibson, "Texas Is Home. The Briggle Family and Their Trans Child Are Fighting for It." *Washington Post*, April 10, 2023. https://www.washingtonpost.com/parenting/2023/04/10/texas-trans-children-families/.

[476] Caitlin Gibson, "Texas Is Home. The Briggle Family and Their Trans Child Are Fighting for It." *Washington Post*, April 10, 2023. https://www.washingtonpost.com/parenting/2023/04/10/texas-trans-children-families/.

[477] All of this is speculation on my part. And I did hear from other parents about Texas families that had lost their transgender children to CPS over charges of child abuse in previous years, although prior to Paxton's opinion or Abbott's new orders. But they were under gag orders and so could only speak privately off the record. I would also hear of other parents in Kansas, Michigan, and South Carolina who had their transgender children taken away from them by their states over charges of child abuse. However, they were unable to speak out because all were apparently under gag orders.

[478] Personal communication with author, Feb 13 2023.

[479] This is also going to reflected in the coming avalanche of badly-worded and overly-broad bills which are about to be introduced in the legislature, which will seek to target nearly every aspect of transgender kids' lives. As transgender Rev. Remington Johnson would explain, "These bills are badly drawn with a purpose: because the more that can be read into them, the more they terrorize parents, who aren't sure what they mean or how they might be used against them. And that drives down the number of families willing to risk providing care to their trans kids." 3

[480] Personal communication with author Feb 14 2023.

[481] "Baker Botts." *Wikipedia*, March 10, 2023. https://en.wikipedia.org/wiki/Baker_Botts.

[482] Lambda Legal. "Doe v. Abbott - Lambda Legal," March 7, 2023. https://www.lambdalegal.org/in-court/cases/doe-v-abbott.

[483] Adam Klasfeld, "Judge Temporarily Shields Family and Psychologist from Texas Governor's Order on Transgender Care for Youth," Law & Crime, March 3, 2022. https://lawandcrime.com/civil-rights/judge-blocks-texas-governors-order-for-family-service-investigations-over-medical-treatment-for-transgender-kids/.

[484] Lauren McGaughy, "Does the State Think Transgender Care Is Abuse? Ken Paxton's Comments Contradict Texas' Legal Stance." *Dallas News*, March 11, 2022. https://www.dallas news.com/news/politics/2022/03/10/does-the-state-think-transgender-care-is-abuse-ken-paxtons-comments-contradict-texas-legal-stance/.

[485] "ACLU Sues Texas for Alleged Investigations of Transgender Kids' Families," March 3, 2022. https://www.nbcnews.com /nbc-out/out-politics-and-policy/judge-blocks-texas-investigation-trans-teens-parents-treatments-rcna18459.

[486] Katelyn Burns, "'When a Child Tells You Who They Are, Believe Them': The Psychologist Taking on Texas' Anti-Trans Policies." *The Guardian*, March 2, 2022. https://www. theguardian.com/world/2022/mar/02/megan-mooney-texas-psychologist-taking-on-anti-trans-policies.

[487] Maggie Haberman, "Businesses Assail Texas Move to Classify Care for Trans Teens as 'Child Abuse.'" *The New York Times*, March 11, 2022. https://www.nytimes.com/ 2022/03/10/us/politics/businesses-texas-trans-teens-child-abuse.html.

[488] All names in italics are legal pseudonyms used in the case.

[489] "Doe v. Abbott - Lambda Legal," March 7, 2023. https://www.lambdalegal.org/in-court/cases/doe-v-abbott.

[490] American Civil Liberties Union. "PFLAG v. Abbott | American Civil Liberties Union," April 20, 2023. https://www.aclu.org/cases/pflag-v-abbott.

[491] The Poe case is among the only known families where the state has acted against the family of a nonbinary child.

[492] American Civil Liberties Union. "Doe v. Abbott | American Civil Liberties Union," April 18, 2023. https://www.aclu.org /cases/doe-v-abbott?document=Petition-for-Writ-of-Mandamus-.

[493] Karen Brooks Harper, "GENECIS Program Can Accept New Patients Seeking Gender-Affirming Care." *The Texas Tribune*, March 24, 2023. https://www.texastribune.org/2022/05/12/transgender-gender-affirming-care-genecis/.

[494] Eleanor Klibanoff, "Texas DFPS Resumes Investigations into Parents of Trans Kids." *The Texas Tribune*, March 24, 2023. https://www.texastribune.org/2022/05/20/trans-texas-child-abuse-investigations/.

[495] Derrick Stuckly, "Texas DFPS Blocked from Investigating Members of PFLAG Giving Their Children Transgender Treatment." *Brownwood News*, September 21, 2022. https://www.brownwoodnews.com/2022/09/21/texas-dfps-blocked-from-investigating-members-of-pflag-giving-their-children-transgender-treatment/.

[496] Judge Meachum, a Democrat up for reelection in November, confirms her original finding on July 8, blocking DFPS from further investigation of plaintiffs *Poe* and *Voe*. That September, she will do the same for the Briggles, as well as for PFLAG and all its Texas members See: American Civil Liberties Union. "PFLAG v. Abbott | American Civil Liberties Union," April 20, 2023. https://www.aclu.org/cases/pflag-v-abbott#legal-documents.

[497] Both trials are still caught in the web of appeals as of this writing, and neither PFLAG's case nor *Jane Doe*s have moved forward, as the state, the ACLU, and Lambda duel over injunctions, with additional appeals always likely.

[498] Lindsey Dawson, Jennifer Kates, and MaryBeth Musueci. "Youth Access to Gender Affirming Care: The Federal and State Policy Landscape," June 13, 2022. https://www.kff.org/other/issue-brief/youth-access-to-gender-affirming-care-the-federal-and-state-policy-landscape/.

[499] By 2023, about half the states had introduced anti-care laws or policies, and 20 in total has put them into effect: Arkansas, Florida, Georgia, Idaho, Indiana, Iowa, Kentucky, Louisiana, Mississippi, Missouri, Montana, Nebraska, North Carolina, North Dakota, Oklahoma, South Dakota, Tennessee, Texas, Utah, West Virginia See: https://www.usnews.com/news/best-states/articles/2023-03-30/what-is-gender-affirming-care-and-which-states-have-restricted-it-in-2023#LA

[500] https://www.themarysue.com/the-right-wants-to-stop-trans-adults-from-transitioning-because-kids-werent-enough/ l

[501] Generally even when far-right judges uphold bans, federal appellate courts has been pretty uniform in recognizing the blatant unconstitutionality of allowing care for cisgender teens while making it illegal for transgender ones. However, in July 2023, the Sixth U.S. Circuit Court of Appeals became the exception, reversing a low court judge's injunction 2-1, , and allowing Tennessee's ban to go into immediately effect. It was a shocking departure, and eventually be heard by the full court later in 2023.

See: https://apnews.com/article/transgender-health-care-tennessee-appeal-reversal-f0bf16e7a508406f50b3bf6d9343313b

[502] Human Rights Campaign, December 6, 2016. https://www.hrc.org/press-releases/new-polling-details-watershed-moment-for-lgbtq-equality-hb2-led-to-pat-mccr.

[503] Azeen Ghorayshi, "Many States Are Trying to Restrict Gender Treatments for Adults, Too." *The New York Times*, April 22, 2023. https://www.nytimes.com/2023/04/22/health/trans gender-adults-treatment-bans.html.

[504] In June, 2023 the Texas House and Senate, having been stripped of the more moderate Republican leadership, would pass an anti-care bill to Abbott's desk. See: https://www.texastribune.org/2023/06/02/texas-gender-affirming-care-ban/

[505] https://time.com/6176799/trans-sports-bans-conservative-movement/

[506] Riki Wilchins and Chloe Souchere, "Analysis of ACLU Transgender legislation," unpublished raw data, 2023 https://www.aclu.org/legislative-attacks-on-lgbtq-rights.

[507] 61% (11) of these organizations spoke out against bathroom bills and about the same number against school sports laws.

[508] Our list, which is a decidedly unscientific sample, included the American Association of University Women (AAUW), Anti-Defamation League (ADL), AFL-CIO, Color of Change, Lawyers Committee for Civil Rights, Legal Momentum, Mexican American Legal Defense and Educational Fund, NAACP & NAACP Legal Defense Fund, National Education Association (NEA), National Partnership for Women and Families, National Urban League, National Council La Raza

(NCLR), National Organization for Women (NOW), National Women's Law Center (NWLC), People for the American Way, Race Forward, Service Employees International Union (SEIU), and Southern Poverty Law Center (SPLC).

[509] In fact, the only organization among the 18 we could find that issued more than a single statement in support of young people's access to affirming care was the National Partnership for Women and Families, with three.

[510] There were about 30 for bathrooms and for sports from these same organization.

[511] https://www.americanprogress.org/article/expanding-access-and-protections-in-states-where-abortion-is-legal/

[512] https://www.reuters.com/article/us-gaymarriage-usa-idUSTRE75O0G420110625

[513] In June, 2022 NACAR would tweet a single apology for letting Abbott wave the starter's flag during a race during Pride month.

[514] It also ensured that federal funds cannot go to conversion therapy, which is not really at issue in most states. He would also ensure that the VA would continue offering affirming care, which neither affects nor helps transkids.

[515] His EO did include a model policy and some support for public education.

[516] Laura Meckler, "Biden Administration Says Schools May Bar Trans Athletes from Competitive Teams." *Washington Post*, April 6, 2023. https://www.washingtonpost.com/education/2023/04/06/trans-athletes-school-sports-title-ix/.

[517] Maegan Vazquez, "Biden Marks International Transgender Day of Visibility by Blasting Republicans Targeting Trans Youth." *CNN*, March 31, 2023. https://www.cnn.com/2023/03/31/politics/biden-transgender-day-of-visibility/index.html.

[518] "Executive Order on Advancing Equality for Lesbian, Gay, Bisexual, Transgender, Queer, and Intersex Individuals." *The White House*, June 15, 2022. https://www.whitehouse.gov/briefing-room/presidential-actions/2022/06/15/executive-order-on-advancing-equality-for-lesbian-gay-bisexual-transgender-queer-and-intersex-individuals/.

[519] Sarah Owermohle and Eugene Daniels, "Biden Launches Plan to Protect Transgender Youths' Health Care," June 15, 2022. https://www.politico.com/news/2022/06/15/biden-plan-transgender-youth-health-care-00039844.

[520] Groups that helped led the legal fight with ACLU and Lambda Legal included the Human Rights Campaign (HRC), GLBTQ Advocates and Defenders (GLAD), the National Center for Lesbian Rights (NCLR), and Southern Legal Counsel.

[521] American Academy of Child and Adolescent Psychiatry, American Academy of Dermatology, American Academy of Family Physicians, American Academy of Nursing, American Academy of Pediatrics, American Academy of Physician Assistants, American College Health Association, American College of Nurse-Midwives, American College of Obstetricians and Gynecologists, American College of Physicians, American Counseling Association, American Heart Association, American Medical Association, American Nurses Association, American Osteopathic Association, American Psychiatric Association, American Psychological Association, American Public Health Association, American Society of Plastic Surgeons, Endocrine Society, National Association of Nurse Practitioners in Women's Health, National Association of Social Workers, National Commission on Correctional Health Care, Pediatric Endocrine Society, Society for Adolescent Health and Medicine, World Medical Association, World Professional Association for Transgender Health.

[522] https://academic.oup.com/jsm/article/20/3/398/7005631?search result=1

[523] https://www.psychologytoday.com/us/blog/political-minds/202201/the-evidence-trans-youth-gender-affirming-medical-care

[524] https://jamanetwork.com/journals/jamasurgery/article-abstract/2808129

[525] "Detransition" rates and "regret rates" are not at all the same. The overwhelming majority of those listed in studies as "detransitioning" did not regret treatment. On the contrary, many of them simply changed their identification, most often trans boy or trans girl to something like nonbinary,

genderqueer, or genderfluid. Others stopped treatment not because they realized they had made a mistake, but because of intense pressure to do so from hostile families or employers or because of relentless bullying and/or social harassment. At least one study found that a 62% of those listed as "detransitioners" actually resumed their transition at a later date. (See https://twitter.com/ErinInTheMorn/status /1513034680802631681?utm_source=substack&utm_mediu m=email) However, unfortunately medical studies seldom if ever code the *reason* for ceasing or altering treatment regimes, nor do they generally do follow-up studies to see if those categorized as doing so eventually resume treatment at a later date.

[526] https://journals.lww.com/annalsplasticsurgery/Abstract/2022/ 05004/Gender_Affirming_Mastectomy_Trends_and_Surgica l.4.aspx

[527] https://www.thelancet.com/journals/lanchi/article/PIIS2352- 4642(22)00254-1/fulltext

[528] https://www.gendergp.com/detransition-facts/

[529] https://nytletter.com

[530] https://www.sfchronicle.com/opinion/article/new-york-times- trans-18214925.php

[531] https://translash.org/transcript-capturing-the-new-york-times/

[532] For instance, see SPLC's write-up of ACP here: https://www. splcenter.org/fighting-hate/extremist-files/group/american- college-pediatricians

[533] "It Is Journalism's Sacred Duty To Endanger The Lives Of As Many Trans People As Possible." *The Onion*, February 17, 2023. https://www.theonion.com/it-is-journalism-s-sacred- duty-to-endanger-the-lives-of-1850126997.

[534] Private conversation with author Jan 5 2023

[535] The Washington Post has been an outstanding exception, carrying lengthy and substantive pieces which poll the trans community and trans youth in particular on their lives and experiences around care and similar issues, while publishing extensive fact-based pieces that which can generally be counted on to be scrupulously even-handed.

[536] While the right now lies obviously and continuously about the most obvious facts—-stolen elections, fake COVID "cures,"

the "dangers" of vaccines—mainstream media has successfully adjusted its coverage of everything except the lies about transgender kids.

[537] https://www.theguardian.com/books/2022/aug/05/michigan-library-book-bans-lgbtq-authors

[538] https://news.sky.com/story/neo-nazi-group-disrupts-drag-story-hour-for-children-in-new-hampshire-12907443

[539] https://www.npr.org/2023/08/20/1194932544/lauri-carleton-california-store-owner-killed-pride-flag-lgbtq

[540] Personal communication with author, April 2023.

[541] "Protect Anne's Kids from Political Extremists, Organized by Rachel Gonzales," Gofundme.com, n.d. https://www.gofundme.com/f/protect-annes-kids-from-political-extremists.

[542] "The Texas GOP's Darling: Jeff Younger." Texas Signal, March 2, 2023. https://texassignal.com/the-texas-gops-darling-jeff-younger/.

[543] Bellan, like Meachum another urban Democrat, was also up for reelection in Dallas County in November of 2022 and won handily See: "Melissa Bellan," Ballotpedia, n.d. https://ballotpedia.org/Melissa_Bellan.

[544] Personal communication with author, Jan 21, 2023.

[545] Deepa Shivaram, "Florida Gov. DeSantis Taps A New Surgeon General Who Doesn't Support Vaccine Mandates." *NPR*, September 22, 2021. https://www.npr.org/2021/09/22/1039613351/desantis-florida-surgeon-general-vaccine-mandates.

[546] H. Holden. Thorp, "Remember, Do No Harm?" *Science* 378, no. 6617 (October 13, 2022): 231. https://doi.org/10.1126/science.adf3072.

[547] In 2023, he will actually be denounced by the CDC and the FDA for his crazy COVID theories.
"Florida Surgeon General's Covid Vaccine Claims Harm Public, Health Agencies Say." *The Guardian*, March 13, 2023. https://www.theguardian.com/us-news/2023/mar/12/florida-surgeon-generals-covid-vaccine-claims-harm-public-health-agencies-warn.

[548] https://www.erininthemorning.com/p/florida-agencies-manipulated-research?utm_source=post-email-title

&publication_id=994764&post_id=121588691&isFreemail=
false&utm_medium=email

549 Technically, Florida didn't ban adult care, but the Medical
Board imposed such a lengthy list of requirements for
adults—including multiple and repeated evaluations and both
medical and psychiatric checkups —that made it impossible
to prescribe or receive care. It also required physicians to
complete a specific form which it very carefully never
actually designed or published. It was the transgender
equivalent of TRAP bills (Targeted Restriction of Abortion
Providers), in which red states imposed long lists of
medically unnecessary and literally impossible requirements
that made abortion technically still legal but for all practical
purposes unavailable.
550 Months later this is finally stayed by the federal courts.
551 Lil Kalish, "Trans Activist Injects Testosterone At Florida
Board Meeting." *BuzzFeed News*, February 13, 2023.
https://www.buzzfeednews.com/article/lilkalish/trans-
activist-injects-testosterone-florida-medicine-
meeting?utm_source=substack&utm_medium=email.
552 The reader should note that other sources, such as Trans
Legislation Tracker and researcher Erin Reed or even the
ACLU itself, may have slightly different numbers than ours
for both bill introduced and passed. We tried to parse out
only those bills that were specifically or at least primarily
directed at transgender people, which was sometimes a
matter of judgment. In addition, bills are often paused and
then restarted, held up in hearings, or rewritten and
reintroduced. So some bills we counted as not passing may
indeed have been enacted into law. So all these numbers
should be considered provisional and approximate rather than
fixed and final.
553 For a slightly different account but with similar numbers, see
the Washington Post's analysis of the same data here:
https://www.washingtonpost.com/dc-md-va/2023/04/17/anti-
trans-bills-map/
554 Guttmacher Institute, which provided this data, did not have It
available for years prior to 2020. Also measures which

sought to restrict reproductive health rights but did not target -abortion specifically are not included.

[555] The Brennan Center for Justice tracks the number of bills introduced, carried over or pre-filed in January of each year. These numbers would be change during the following 11 months.

[556] https://www.guttmacher.org/article/2020/12/state-policy-trends-2020-reproductive-health-and-rights-year-no-other

[557] https://www.guttmacher.org/article/2021/12/state-policy-trends-2021-worst-year-abortion-rights-almost-half-century

[558] https://www.brennancenter.org/our-work/research-reports/voting-laws-roundup-february-2023

[559] https://www.guttmacher.org/2022/12/state-policy-trends-2022-devastating-year-us-supreme-courts-decision-overturn-roe-leads

[560] https://www.brennancenter.org/our-work/research-reports/voting-laws-roundup-february-2023

[561] This is an approximate number provided by the Guttmacher Institute's media office in an email dated April 25, 2023.

[562] https://www.brennancenter.org/our-work/research-reports/voting-laws-roundup-february-2023

[563] Robin Respaut and Chad Terhune, Reuters. "Number of Transgender Children Seeking Treatment Surges in U.S.," October 6, 2022. https://www.reuters.com/investigates/special-report/usa-transyouth-data/.

[564] Being transgender used to be considered a psychiatric disorder called Gender Identity Disorder; The American Psychiatric Association has since changed this to mental health condition called Gender Dysphoria, which is diagnosed for the *distress* some trans people feel because of the incongruence between their inner gender identity and their bodies, instead of pathologizing being transgender or being gender nonconforming *per se.* For instance, See: https://www.glaad.org/blog/apa-removes-gender-identity-disorder-updated-mental-health-guide

[565] The disparity between the numbers may be because blockers are often used to delay hormone treatment in order to provide children and their families more time to consider their

situation. Also some youth go straight to hormones, without first taking blockers.

566 Casey Parks, Emily Guskin, and Scott Clement, "Most Trans Adults Say Transitioning Made Them More Satisfied with Their Lives." *Washington Post*, March 23, 2023. https://www.washingtonpost.com/dc-md-va/2023/03/23/ transgender-adults-transitioning-poll/.

567 Riki Wilchins, "Do Trans Teens Have Rights to Their Bodies? (Then Why Won't We Say So…)." *Medium*, January 2, 2023. https://medium.com/@rikiwilchins/do-trans-kid-have-rights-to-their-bodies-then-why-wont-we-say-so-b0e78e6e0506.

568 Washington state has a bill pending which would allow minors as young as 13 to receive affirming mental health and medical care without parental consent in some circumstances. California is also considering a law that would do similarly in specific situations, such as foster care. And in July, 2023 Maine would pass a law allowing 16- and 17-year-old to consent to affirming care without parental permission. See: https://www.mainepublic.org/politics/2023-07-12/maine-expands-ability-of-older-teens-to-receive-gender-affirming-care-without-parents-consent

569 Jody L. Herman, Andrew R. Flores, & Kathryn K. O'Neill, "How Many Adults and Youth Identify as Transgender in the United States? - Williams Institute." Williams Institute, September 27, 2022. https://williamsinstitute.law.ucla.edu/publications/trans-adults-united-states/

**Other Riverdale Avenue Books/
Magnus Titles You Might Like
By Riki Wilchins**

*When Loving Your Kid is a Crime:
Parents of Transgender Children Speak Out*

*TRANS/Gressive:
How Transgender Activists Took on Gay Rights,
Feminism, the Media and Congress*

*Burn the Binary:
Selected Writings on the Politics of Trans-
Genderqueer and Nonbinary*

Gender Queer: Voices from Beyond the Sexual Binary

*Read My Lips:
Sexual Subversion and the End of Gender*

Queer Theory, Gender Theory: An Instant Primer

Books from Other Authors Published by Riverdale Avenue Books You Might Like

Hiding in Plain Sight
By Zane Thimmesch-Gill

Finding Masculinity:
Female to Male Transition in Adulthood
Edited by Alexander Walker and Emmett J.P. Lundberg

Outside the XY:
Queer, Black and Brown Masculinity
Edited by Brooklyn Boihood

Queering Sexual Violence:
Radical Voices from Within the Anti-Violence Movement
Edited by Jennifer Patterson

Two Spirits, One Heart:
A Mother, Her Transgender Son
and their Journey to Love and Acceptance
By Marsha and Aiden Aizumi